IT'S IN THE CARDS

IT'S IN THE CARDS

♣ ♥ ♠ ♦

MARTHY JONES

SAMUEL WEISER, INC.

York Beach, Maine

First published in 1984 by
Samuel Weiser, Inc.
Box 612
York Beach, Maine 03910

99 98
12 11 10 9 8 7

Library of Congress Catalog Card Number: 84-50135

ISBN 0-87728-600-0
MV

Our gratitude to the translator, Jeanet Breen.
Cards used to illustrate the cover are from the Baroque Bridge
Deck, published by Piatnik Playing Cards, Vienna. Cards used
to illustrate the text are reprinted by permission of Heraclio
Fournier, Vitoria, Spain. Both decks are distributed exclusively
in the United States of America by US Games Systems, Inc.,
179 Ludlow St., Stamford, CT 06902.

Printed in the United States of America

The paper used in this publication meets the minimum require-
ments of the American National Standard for Permanence of
Paper for Printed Library Materials Z39.48-1984.

CONTENTS

NOTE TO THE READER

This book can help you learn to read the past and future from an ordinary deck of playing cards. When your friends discover your interest, you'll be asked to read at parties and gatherings. The cards can tell you so much about the people that you read for that your "client" may discuss problems in greater depth than you can imagine now.

It is wise to remember that we all are ultimately self-responsible. We cannot make any major life decisions for someone else. We can be of service by pointing out certain situations illustrated by the cards, but don't try to make anyone change. Avoid making final decisions for others. It's hard enough trying to recognize our own motives, let alone those of a stranger. Handle this knowledge with care, and you'll develop your intuition in ways that may astound you in years to come.

The author

PART I
LEARNING TO READ
THE CARDS

INTRODUCTION

No two card readers interpret the cards in exactly the same way, but most base their interpretations on the traditional values associated with the cards. Many enthusiasts have puzzled over the origin of traditional meanings for the cards, trying to uncover the logic upon which this system was based. It is perhaps of interest to mention the most common explanations for the existence of the traditional interpretations.

The most remarkable is the suggestion that a relationship exists between the cards and the calendar year. The reasoning for this is as follows: the pack has twelve picture cards (three in each suit) in accordance with the twelve months of the year and the twelve signs of the zodiac. The pack has two colors—red (hearts and diamonds) and black (clubs and spades)—just as the year is divided into two parts by the summer solstice and the equinox. It is also commonly accepted that the four suits of the deck are equivalent to the four seasons of the year.

In addition, each suit consists of thirteen cards corresponding with the thirteen weeks in each season. There are twelve complete lunar cycles in each year and the pack consists of 52 cards corresponding with the fifty-two weeks in the year.

Further points of correspondence were found between the number of days in the year and the cards as follows: if the point value of each card is added up, with the aces counting as 1, kings, queens and jacks respectively as 13, 12, and 11, a total of 364 is obtained. The addition of the joker equals 365. This corresponds to the number of days in the year. If we add up the individual numbers contained in 364 (3 + 6 + 4), the result is 13, the numbers of cards in a suit!

The thirteen values of each card in one suit can be added together and the total is 91, or the length of a season. If we divide 91 by 7 (the number of days in a week), we again obtain 13. The sum of the separate figures 1 + 3 = 4, which is both the number of the seasons and the suits of the deck. The numbers 13 and 7 appear to have the same importance here as with the tarot cards.

A similar operation can be performed on the number of letters in the names of the cards of one suit. For example:

> In *German*: (ch is one letter) as, zwei, drei, vier, fünf, sechs, sieben, acht, neun, zehn, dube, dame, könig = 52!

> In *French*: un, deux, trois, quatre, cinq, six, sept, huit, neuf, dix, valet, reine, roi = 52!

> In *Dutch*: (ij is one letter) aas, twee, drie, vier, vijf, zes, zeven, acht, negen, tien, boer, vrouw, heer = 52!

> In *English*: ace, two, three, four, five, six, seven, eight, nine, ten, jack, queen, king = 52!

We could cite still more elaborate examples to support this concept, but the details mentioned above should be sufficiently convincing for anyone interested in these theories.

LAYING OUT THE CARDS FOR A READING

There are several basic things that have to be done before you can do a reading. You have to get your deck ready; you need to find a comfortable position for you and your client; you have to pick a personal card that represents your client.

First you need a deck of cards. Most card readers have their own deck that they use all the time. Because this deck may have been used by many people, you want to clear it of any vibrations it may hold from the last person who used it. To do this, you simply run your hands through the deck and shuffle it yourself. This cleans the deck and readies both you and the cards for the next person's vibrations. Should you use a deck that is given to you by someone else, do the same thing. The important thing here is to get the old vibrations off, and to get yourself tuned into what you are about to do.

When you do a reading, you will be looking at where the cards are positioned in the spread. As you read this book, you will be referred to the upper right or left of a particular spread, as the card's position (whether in the upper right or left, whether right side up or reversed) will influence the reading. For this reason, you may wish to sit next to your client, so as to better interpret any changes in meaning. It will help your concentration if you consider the physical space you need before you start.

DETERMINING THE PERSONAL CARD

The first thing you need to do before you can begin laying out the cards for a reading is to determine the personal card that symbolizes your client. This is something that you, as the reader, must do and there are two basic ways to do this. Traditionally, the designation of the personal card has been fulfilled by the picture cards, as follows:

> King and Queen of Clubs: people with brown hair and brown eyes
> King and Queen of Hearts: people with dark blond hair and gray eyes
> King and Queen of Spades: people with a dark appearance
> King and Queen of Diamonds: people with blond or red hair

You may find, however, that these descriptions or "types" do not easily fit your client—you can, in such an instance, choose the personal card based on the date of birth, as shown in Figure 1 on page 6. In order to use this list, you need to know the birth *day*—not the year—of your client, and the card can be picked from the list. For example, if someone is born on March 15th, use the seven of clubs. For someone born on February 4th, use the four of hearts.

Now that the personal card has been chosen, extract it from the deck and give the remaining cards to your client to shuffle. Shuffling should take place quietly and thoughtfully, and

	Jan.	Feb.	Mar.	April	May	June	July	Aug.	Sept.	Oct.	Nov.	Dec.
1	Q♦	4♠	6♥	Joker	A♦	6♠	10♥	2♣	7♦	J♠	3♥	7♣
2	K♦	5♠	7♥	J♣	2♦	7♠	J♥	3♣	8♠	Q♠	4♥	8♣
3	A♦	6♠	8♥	Q♣	3♦	8♠	Q♥	4♣	9♦	K♠	5♥	9♣
4	2♦	7♠	9♥	K♣	4♦	9♠	K♥	5♣	10♦	A♠	6♥	10♣
5	3♦	8♠	10♥	A♣	5♦	10♠	A♥	6♣	J♦	2♠	7♥	J♣
6	4♦	9♠	J♥	2♣	6♦	J♠	2♥	7♣	Q♦	3♠	8♥	Q♣
7	5♦	10♠	Q♥	3♣	7♦	Q♠	3♥	8♣	K♦	4♠	9♥	K♣
8	6♦	J♠	K♥	4♣	8♦	K♠	4♥	9♣	A♦	5♠	10♥	A♣
9	7♦	Q♠	A♥	5♣	9♦	A♠	5♥	10♣	2♦	6♠	J♥	2♣
10	8♦	K♠	2♥	6♣	10♦	2♠	6♥	J♣	3♦	7♠	Q♥	3♣
11	9♦	A♠	3♥	7♣	J♦	3♠	7♥	Q♣	4♦	8♠	K♥	4♣
12	10♦	2♠	4♥	8♣	Q♦	4♠	8♥	K♣	5♦	9♠	A♥	5♣
13	J♦	3♠	5♥	9♣	K♦	5♠	9♥	A♣	6♦	10♠	2♥	6♣
14	Q♦	4♠	6♥	10♣	A♦	6♠	10♥	2♣	7♦	J♠	3♥	7♣
15	K♦	5♠	7♥	J♣	2♦	7♠	J♥	3♣	8♦	Q♠	4♥	8♣
16	A♦	6♥	8♥	Q♣	3♦	8♠	Q♥	4♣	9♦	K♠	5♥	9♣
17	2♦	7♠	9♥	K♣	4♦	9♠	K♥	5♣	10♦	A♠	6♥	10♣
18	3♦	8♠	10♥	A♣	5♦	10♠	A♥	6♣	J♦	2♠	7♥	J♣
19	4♦	9♥	J♥	2♣	6♦	J♠	2♥	7♣	Q♦	3♠	8♥	Q♣
20	5♦	10♥	Q♥	3♣	7♦	Q♠	3♥	8♣	K♦	4♠	9♥	K♣
21	6♠	J♥	K♥	4♦	8♠	K♠	4♥	9♣	A♠	5♠	10♥	A♦
22	7♠	Q♥	A♣	5♦	9♠	A♥	5♥	10♣	2♠	6♠	J♥	2♦
23	8♠	K♥	2♣	6♦	10♠	2♥	6♣	J♣	3♠	7♠	Q♣	3♦
24	9♠	A♥	3♣	7♦	J♠	3♥	7♣	Q♦	4♠	8♥	K♣	4♦
25	10♠	2♥	4♣	8♦	Q♠	4♥	8♣	K♦	5♠	9♥	A♣	5♦
26	J♠	3♥	5♣	9♦	K♠	5♥	9♣	A♦	6♠	10♥	2♣	6♦
27	Q♠	4♥	6♣	10♦	A♠	6♥	10♣	2♦	7♠	J♥	3♣	7♦
28	K♠	5♥	7♣	J♦	2♠	7♥	J♣	3♦	8♠	Q♥	4♣	8♦
29	A♠	Joker	8♣	Q♦	3♠	8♥	Q♣	4♦	9♠	K♥	5♣	9♦
30	2♠		9♣	K♦	4♠	9♥	K♣	5♦	10♠	A♥	6♣	10♦
31	3♠		10♣		5♠		A♣	6♦		2♥		J♦

Figure 1. The correspondences between the cards and the days of the year. The column on the left shows the days of the month. The months of the year are listed across the top of the table. In order to find the card that rules the day in question, read across to find the month you need, and down to find the day. For example, a person born on October 15th would be ruled by the Queen of Spades. Someone born on July 6th is ruled by the Two of Hearts.

should be done for some time. Each person who shuffles will do it differently, as some people will automatically shuffle the cards for quite a while, and others just won't. Don't let your client shuffle the cards by dividing them into two stacks on the table and intermixing them with a movement of the thumbs— this kind of shuffling should be reserved for card games. It is more important that the cards be shuffled the old-fashioned way, from hand to hand, as the cards can then pick up the circumstances of the client.

THE BASIC 52 CARD READING

A card reading answers questions for your client. You, as the card reader, are the vehicle for those answers through the technique of laying out the cards. When you begin reading for others, be prepared for a wide variety of possible questions— some may be very specific questions ("Will I get a raise next month?") and some may be very vague ("What's going to happen in my life?"). Later in this section we will look at how to use specific layouts for specific types of questions and circumstances. But keep in mind that if there is good contact between the reader and the client, the technique used for laying out the cards is of minor importance.

The basic 52 card reading is the most popular among the gypsies because it is an easy one to remember. It is a 15 card layout, and may appear extremely simple, but there are 7,921,834,931,684,532,415,560,000 possible variations. The chance of repetition is so infinitely small as to be negligible!

Figure 2 on page 8 shows the order in which the cards should be laid out. Begin by placing the personal card in the center of the layout, in position number 1. Now have your client shuffle the cards again and when they are done, hand the deck back to you. Draw the top card, or hold the deck out to the client so that a card can be drawn at random. (Some readers allow the client to choose all of the cards for the reading—let your intuition tell you how you wish to handle the choosing of the cards.) This card is placed in position number 2. Remember that you are the one who places the cards on the table, as they have to be put in the correct positions.

Top Left-Hand Corner

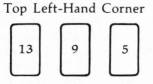

The future. The possibility
of choice or adjustment.

Top Right-Hand Corner

The future.
Natural development

Center

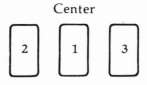

The client.
The client's immediate
problems or circumstances

Bottom Left-Hand Corner

Elements from the past
which influence the future.
An influence in a decision.

Bottom Right-Hand Corner

Circumstances and influences
over which the client has no
control. An influence in a
decision.

Figure 2. The basic and most popular layout using a deck of 52
cards. Fifteen cards should be laid out according to the positions
shown here.

Have your client shuffle the cards again. You either again take the top card, or allow your client to draw from the deck. This card goes in position number 3. Repeat this process until you have laid out 15 cards in the sequence shown in Figure 2. You are now ready to read the cards. You won't need the rest of the deck.

Keep in mind that no card has any value in total isolation. A card is always influenced by the layout as a whole, and by its adjacent cards in particular. Before you have the whole layout to survey, don't comment on the individual cards.

HOW TO READ THE BASIC LAYOUT

You now have five basic groups of cards to read. We will discuss each section by itself, but first it is important to understand the basic interpretation of where the cards are placed. This list can be easily memorized.

Center Position: The client, the problems and circumstances

Upper Left: The future—its choices and possibilities for adjustment

Upper Right: The future—its natural development

Lower Left: The past—how it influences the future

Lower Right: The influences outside the client

We start at the center (the card in position number 1 in Figure 2) as it represents the client. Look at this card to determine the client's personality. This card will also tell you something about the nature of the problems surrounding the client, or the influences which may be considered *disturbing* to the client at this time in life. You know what the cards mean. The client may or may not tell you why the reading is desired, so this card is very important to understand, as it signifies the "feeling" around the reading. It is further influenced by the cards on either side, so the next thing to do is to observe which cards are sitting in positions 2 and 3 in the spread. These cards provide additional information about the client's situation. If you see a picture card in the center section of the spread, it may further symbolize the client in a personal sense, or it may represent a person close to the client. The latter is particularly true when the picture card signifies a person of the opposite sex.

Move on to the upper right hand corner. These cards (in positions 4, 8, and 12) indicate the direction your client's life is taking if nothing is done to change its course. As you listen to your client, keep this section in mind. One of the advantages of having the cards read is that the reading brings an opportunity for change. Nothing is "in the cards" if the client is willing to make some adjustments in the present life style, for these adjustments change the future.

The cards in the upper left hand corner (in positions 13, 9, and 5) indicate that the client may take another path. The cards will indicate whether or not this path is dangerous.

By looking at the cards above the client, you are actually looking into the future. The cards symbolize the directions that could be taken. This is where a reading can be of value, for you can mention the qualities and opportunities symbolized by the cards you see there, and warn the client of things that could cause problems later on. You can also see how the client could change to work within the circumstances that seem to be happening at this moment in time.

The cards in the bottom left-hand corner (in positions 14, 10, and 6) are general indicators of what factors or people are available to help the client make a decision. If your client is over fifty, these cards frequently refer to elements from the past which influence present or future circumstances. In the case of a younger client, the information is more direct, as the elements from the "past" may not have been there too long. This is the section that will tell you how the client can best prepare for upcoming events, as the cards will tell you about the circumstances or ideas that have formed the basis for the client's present position.

The cards lying in the bottom right hand corner (positions 7, 11, and 15) represent external forces. These are forces over which the client has no control, but which can be used to good advantage if handled properly.

The cards that lie under the client are the cards that are used when the client needs to make a decision about something. It is these cards that tell you what the client has put into the situation that presently needs to be handled. It is important to note the good background, as well as the background that has caused the present problem to develop.

AN EXAMPLE LAYOUT

Before going further, let's get an impression from an example layout (or spread) using the 52 card deck for a reading. Figure 3 shows a reading for a young actress who came to consult the cards at a critical point in her career. The advice given by the cards in this situation is particularly clear-cut. The card in the center (position 1) represents the client. It is the jack of diamonds. In position 3 (to the right of the jack) is a three of diamonds, often the symbol of a contract or a chance to do business. On the left of the jack (in position 2) is the ace of clubs, a card of talent and dynamism.

These 3 cards form the central section of the layout, and indicate the client herself. In order to say more about the character and personality of this young actress, you should look up the jack of diamonds (see page 171). By consulting the section dealing with the ace of clubs (see page 62), you will get a clearer impression of the young woman's natural talents. If these two

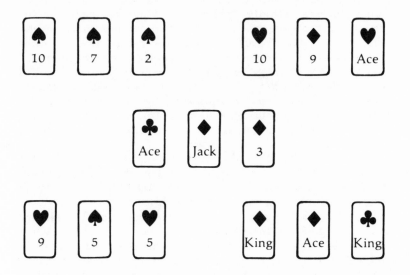

Figure 3. A sample layout for a young actress, using the basic 52 card deck.

cards are interpreted together, they give a portrait of the actress, and it is justifiable to suppose that there is a good chance for her to develop her gifts.

Now look at the top right-hand corner. All the cards in this section are favorable. She has the ten of hearts, the nine of diamonds and the ace of hearts here. If you look these cards up in Part III, you will see that they indicate prosperity, fame, success, happiness and the attainment of some kind of goal in life. This corner represents the normal course of the young actress's life. The advice seems to be that she should continue on her current path so that a rich harvest may be gathered in.

Going to the upper left-hand corner, we see that another path lies open to her. Here she has the ten of spades, the seven of spades and the two of spades. Look up the general description of the suits in Part II as well as the cards in Part III. If she moves along this path, the chances are it will lead to failure. This is a warning that cannot be misconstrued. If she doesn't make use of her energy in the direction she has chosen, but allows herself to be influenced by petty quarrels, nitpicking, or resentments, she will probably stray from the path of success. The two of spades indicates a stumbling block, which may not be important in itself, but can have disastrous results if not approached in the right manner. The seven of spades is a card that signifies dissension and it warns the client against discouragement or hasty steps. Combining these two factors with the ten of spades adds to the situation, as this ten indicates that a lack of concentration on projects requiring lengthy preparation will end in unnecessary failure or disappointment. Taking all three cards in this section together, we can easily see how she could choose to move, if she isn't careful.

The bottom right-hand corner gives us clues regarding the outside influences which have control over the young actress's life. We see the ace of diamonds flanked by 2 kings. In order to interpret this section, you will want to look up the individual cards in Part III, but also look at the section called The Picture Cards on page 36 at the end of Part I. The ace of diamonds is a constructive card which often means success on the stage or in the field of fine arts. A king generally represents one particular man, but when 2 kings are so close together, it can indicate a group of men. The conclusion to be drawn here is that a number of men are closely linked with the client, and these men will help her on the road to success. Since the cards in the bottom right are connected with the center by means of a business card (the three of diamonds in position 3), these men should not be looked at in a romantic light, but rather as business contacts.

The cards in the bottom left-hand corner indicate that not everything will run smoothly. In card positions 14, 10, and 6 we have the nine of hearts, the five of spades and the five of hearts. The 2 fives suggest that slight setbacks, tears, disappointments, and times of fear and doubt have taken place. The nine of hearts at the end of the group of 3 signifies that if the client faces her difficulties with determination and courage, she will enjoy more happiness than she might dare to expect.

After looking at the cards individually and together in the five basic groups, you should determine which suit predominates. In this example, the suits are quite evenly distributed, so no further attention needs to be paid to this issue. However, as you count the suits in other readings, always base the count on a final number of 15, and then look up the predominant suit in Part I, to determine the vibration of the reading.

You will also want to determine how many cards have the same value in the spread—how many twos, threes, or tens. This factor is discussed further on in Part I, as high and low cards, suits, and picture cards all change a reading somewhat when they predominate a layout. In our example, there are 3 aces— the ace of clubs, diamonds and hearts. When 3 aces are also accompanied by 2 kings, you have a sign of unexpected difficulties, as well as great activity, radical changes, success, fame, and the chance of unrestrained contacts with a number of people in influential positions.

This general assessment of a reading is quite easy to do. Once you understand the basic meanings of the suits, the numbers, each card in the deck, and what it means to have a predominance of suits, high or low cards, or picture cards, the information is quite easy to assemble. The next challenge is more difficult, for you must listen to your client to find out exactly what he or she is really looking for from the reading. Not everyone will be honest and direct about what is desired. The next sticky-wickett is how to convey this information to your client so it can be used to its maximum advantage.

The client used in this example has achieved one success after another. She is fully aware that there have been many moments when underhanded intrigue could have destroyed her. By discussing all the possibilities with her, she has been able to better use her time, and to spend it where it has been able to do her the most good.

GYPSY 32 CARD READINGS

The beliefs held by the gypsies were often contradictory to other kinds of card interpretations. They frequently made simple, noncommittal pronouncements, which could be easily applied to any situation if you had a little imagination. They often worked with a 32 card deck, using the picture cards as the personal significator for the person read for. When working with the 32 card deck, you must remove all the twos through sixes inclusive from the regular deck. Then use the aces, and all the other cards from the sevens through the kings.

The picture cards were considered very important. The kings and queens were used as personal cards (*i.e.*, representing the person read for) and these have already been mentioned on page 5. Jacks were always considered to be translators (or informers, or even traitors) of the thoughts of the kings and queens of the same suit. This information can be used today, for if you pick a king or queen to represent your client, the jack in that suit may tell you what the client is thinking that has not been told to you. Understanding the jacks can make you a very good card reader.

Jacks were also considered to represent messengers of some sort. The *jack of clubs* could represent a schoolboy or a student. The *jack of diamonds* could be a cadet (or someone from a private or military school), a young soldier, a messenger, or even the postman. The *jack of hearts* is obviously a lover, a mate, a very good girlfriend or boyfriend. The *jack of spades* can be an errand boy, but he also could be an enemy.

The gypsies work with two kinds of interpretation when looking at the cards. If the card is right side up, it is read one way. If it is reversed (or upside-down), it is read another. In order to know which cards are reversed, you will have to mark them in one corner. You determine how the deck should look to you. Either cut one corner on the bottom, or mark it in some way, so when you read the cards you will know which ones are upside-down. A reversed card indicates that the energy of the card may not be used in its most productive or positive way. Conversely, any card description referring to a "negative" factor will usually describe someone with reversed cards.

For example, the ace of clubs usually means good luck, favorable news, and a chance of coming into some money. When the ace is reversed, it signifies good news which will be short lived or delayed. It can also mean that the client will receive some kind of correspondence of an unpleasant nature.

SIGNIFICANCE OF THE 32 CARD DECK

This section provides a short list of the typical gypsy interpretations for the 32 card deck. A complete discussion of suits and numbers appears in Part II, and each card (the complete deck of 52 cards) is described in Part III. The most popular gypsy 32 card layouts will follow.

Ace of Clubs:	Luck; good news; receipt of money, letters or newspapers *Reverse*: good news but the happiness will be of short duration; letters are delayed
King of Clubs:	A good character; loyal *Reverse*: plans can lead to nothing
Queen of Clubs:	A dark friendly woman *Reverse*: untrustworthy; frivolous
Jack of Clubs:	Attractive young man *Reverse*: a good-for-nothing
Ten of Clubs:	A journey or trip; successful and pleasant events *Reverse*: slight misfortunes; trip over water; a train trip near a body of water
Nine of Clubs:	Unexpected stroke of good luck; pleasure; legal matters *Reverse*: small gift; delays; disturbing event; inconveniences; low spirits
Eight of Clubs:	Favorable acquaintances; love; money; happiness; pleasant relationship with friends *Reverse*: difficulties in love; difficulties in regard to news, papers, documents, discussions

Seven of Clubs: Success; some illustrious deed or performance; plans carried into effect; financial investment in some small concern
Reverse: Annoyances concerning money matters; difficulties or complications in legal questions

Ace of Hearts: A house; pleasant news; a cordial or a love letter
Reverse: a change of domicile; a visit from a friend

King of Hearts: An affectionate person of blond appearance
Reverse: disappointment in connection with this person

Queen of Hearts: A loving blond woman
Reverse: unhappy love in connection with this woman

Jack of Hearts: A cheerful young man, perhaps a child
Reverse: disappointment or misfortune; a soldier

Ten of Hearts: Very favorable; good fortune, love, cheerfulness; this mitigates and modifies the significance of any neighboring card
Reverse: birth, change, pleasure, enthusiasm

Nine of Hearts: The wish card; fulfillment of a wish, success and pleasure
Reverse: great affection; someone of whom you are fond; passing difficulties

Eight of Hearts: Love from a blond person; friends, marriage, invitations, clothes, furniture, cordiality
Reverse: unrequited love, jealousy

Seven of Hearts: Cheerful moods and thoughts; some small pleasure or a wish fulfilled; servants or household matters
Reverse: annoyances, disturbed feelings, unnecesary fuss or excitement, concern about nothing; moodiness

Ace of Spades: Feelings of satisfaction and gratification; a large building; business affairs
Reverse: worry, sad news, danger, fear, death

King of Spades: An untrustworthy, dark man
Reverse: a dangerous enemy

Queen of Spades: A widow or an older woman
Reverse: a malevolent old woman

Jack of Spades: A young man; a student of medicine or law; unfavorable
Reverse: a dangerous, untrustworthy young man

Ten of Spades: Loss and sorrow; loss of freedom; distance, water, a journey
Reverse: passing difficulties, illness, serious loss, people in mourning

Nine of Spades: Loss; thwarted plans and hopes; grief; failure; a bad omen
Reverse: sorrow or misfortune for someone known to your client; serious danger, death, many difficulties

Eight of Spades: Expected disappointments; low spirits; night
Reverse: a broken promise or appointment; uncertainty; melancholy; obstacles; sorrow; disappointment; deceit; conspiracy

Seven of Spades: Anxious suspense; a new decision to be implemented; changes, arrangements, decisions
Reverse: intrigues or foolish undertakings regarding love; upsets; disturbances, nervousness, accidents

Ace of Diamonds: A letter; proposal of marriage; a gift, valuables; paper money
Reverse: financial news, letters or financial matters which cause anxiety

King of Diamonds: Someone with fair or gray hair, perhaps a soldier
Reverse: deceit or treachery in connection with this person

Queen of Diamonds: A blond woman who cannot keep secrets
Reverse: difficulties caused by the malevolence of this person

Jack of Diamonds: A young man in a subordinate position
Reverse: untrustworthy; this man may cause difficulties

Ten of Diamonds: Money, a journey or change of abode
Reverse: problems in connection with or as a result of the above

Nine of Diamonds: Difficulties in connection with a wish; sudden events; anger; sharp objects; firearms
Reverse: danger; fights; pain; if other spades are involved, this card can mean discord between members of the family or with loved ones, or it can indicate serious danger, death, a coffin

Eight of Diamonds: A road, walk or a short trip; a love affair
Reverse: difficulties in love; dissipation; irritation; unpleasantness, things which go wrong, coarse or rude behavior

Seven of Diamonds: Annoying or unfriendly remarks in
connection with a child, brother, sister,
animal or an object
Reverse: a gift, a photo, a parcel; scandal
—not far-reaching, but with serious
consequences

SOME 32 CARD LAYOUTS

Practice will show that some methods of reading the cards
are more successful than others. Sometimes one type of layout
will be more efficient than another, and you can determine this
after listening to why your client wants to have a reading. The
52 card reading works well at a party, as does the 32 card Four
Fan layout. If your client wants to know the timing of a certain
event, you may choose to do the reading using the Four Jack
layout. Keep in mind that the following layouts are all based on
the 32 card deck. (To get 32 cards, we remove all the cards two
through six, remember?)

BASIC GYPSY 32 CARD READING

Have your client shuffle the cards. When the client is done,
take the deck and divide it into 3 stacks. Read the top 3 cards
(the top card in each stack). These 3 cards will tell you what is
surrounding your client right now, and what is really the issue
that needs to be solved. Now that you know the issues
surrounding the reading, replace the three cards where they
belong, and put the cards back where they were. The easiest
way to do this might be to lay the three stacks in order on the
table. Turn the top card over in stack 1, 2, and 3. When you are
finished reading these 3 cards, turn them face down on the
stack they were taken from. Let stack 3 stay on the bottom, put
stack 2 on top of it and replace stack 1 on the very top. It is really
important that you do not disturb the original order of the
cards, for if you do, the entire reading will be confused. This is
important because you have not finished the reading.

As soon as the deck is back in order, divide the cards into 8
stacks of 4 cards. You do this by placing 8 cards face down in a
row on the table—1, 2, 3, 4, 5, 6, 7, 8. Next, lay out the ninth
card on top of card 1, the tenth card on top of card 2, still face

down, until you have laid out all the cards. You are working with a 32 card deck, so this will work out to 4 cards in each of the 8 stacks. Ask your client to pick the stack that he or she feels would best rule the following catagories:

1. Self
2. Wishes
3. A best friend
4. Home
5. Things that must be done
6. Things that must be avoided
7. Things that must take place
8. Chances for success

It doesn't matter which stack your client picks to rule what. However, you must remember which stack is picked to rule what! In the beginning, you may wish to write it down.

When the stacks have been appropriately designated, ar-range them in the order listed above. Pick up each stack separately and in three combinations. Remember, we said that no card can stand by itself in an interpretation? Well, no stack can stand by itself either. Keep in mind how each stack is influenced by the next. We will compare stack 1 with stack 2; stack 2 with stack 3; and stack 3 with stack 4. Each group of 4 cards will be treated the same way.

When you look at stack 2, for example, the four cards in the stack will tell a story about the client's wishes. When you look at stack 1, you will see how the client views himself, and those cards will relate to what is wished for. When you look at stack 3, you will see how the client views his best friend, and how the best friend relates to the client's wishes. After looking at the cards involved, if you know what the cards mean, you will begin to see a picture. It is interesting, for you, as a reader, may pick up on situations that you never dreamed existed. When you pick up on a situation that the client doesn't dream exists, and when that client goes home and deals with the ensuing situation, you may find yourself getting a number of compliments.

This is essentially the easiest and fastest 32 card reading. You will have to develop your knowledge so you know the cards backwards and forwards. As you develop your skills, you may find that certain cards take on a special meaning or nuance to you. This is perfectly acceptable. Gypsy tradition says, "The oracle speaks to every fortune-teller in his own language."

CIRCLE OF TEN

This is another simple way of doing a reading using the 32 card deck. Ask your client to choose a card from the deck. This card represents the client and will influence the reading. Then shuffle the rest of the cards (31). The client may shuffle the cards if he chooses. If not, make sure that the client holds them in his hands for a few moments before you proceed. Hold the 31 cards loosely in your hands so the client can draw three of them. Place the first three cards drawn by the client face down on position number 1. To see how this is done, look at Figure 4 on page 22. Draw three more cards and place them on Position number 2 and so on until all ten positions are laid out. If the client prefers, the cards may be drawn one at a time instead of in groups of three. This is a matter of personal taste and intuition, and will not change the outcome of the reading.

In order to read the cards, you must follow the sequence provided below. This is important, for in the Basic Gypsy Reading the client can pick which pile of cards rules which category of life. In this reading, the sequence *must* remain the same. Read the cards as follows:

Position 1: the client
Position 2: the client's home
Position 3: friends
Position 4: endeavors
Position 5: financial affairs
Position 6: pleasure
Position 7: possible disasters
Position 8: present circumstances
Position 9: the future
Position 10: wishes and desires

The thirty-first card will remain after the cards have been laid out. Put this last card in the middle of the circle of cards, as shown in Figure 4. This card will greatly influence the client and also the outcome of the reading. If it is a picture card, it indicates a person who has, or who will have, great influence on the client's life. If it is the ten of hearts, an ace of clubs, or a nine of hearts, it has a favorable meaning. If, on the contrary, the nine of spades is the last card, it can indicate delays and disappointments, even if the rest of the reading is generally positive. Whatever the particulars of the cards, keep in mind that each position must be read in terms of the other.

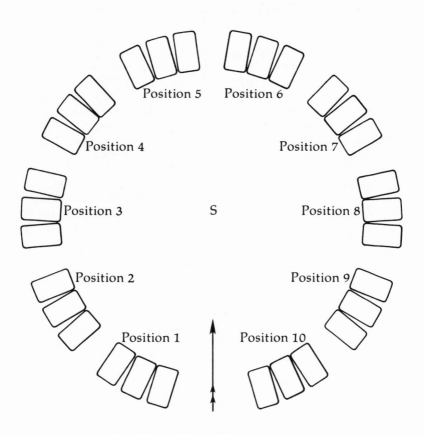

Figure 4. The Circle of Ten. This reading is done using a 32 card deck. The S in the middle of the spread is the personal card or significator that represents the client.

THE FOUR FANS

This is the layout used by most gypsies when they read for many people in a short period of time, so you may want to use this particular format when doing readings at a party. It takes a very short time to read this way, and the reading provides a great deal of information.

Have your client shuffle the cards for some time and then hand them to you. Hold them loosely, face down, in your hands while the client draws 8 cards at random from the pack. Before asking the client to draw the cards, let it be known that the cards can be drawn one at a time or in groups, and this decision is the client's choice. Drawing the cards is really an intuitive reaction on the part of the person you read for.

Place the first batch of 8 cards face up in the form of a fan, beginning in the lower left-corner, as shown in Figure 5 on page 24. The cards must be laid out in exactly the same order as they were chosen by the client. Then have the client draw 8 more cards—still allowing your client to choose whether or not to take the cards one at a time or in groups. This second batch will be laid out above the cards presently lying in Position 1. Once the second batch is laid out, the client chooses the cards for Position 3. These cards are placed to the right of position Number 2 in your layout. The fourth batch (or the remaining cards in the pack of 32) will be laid to the right of Position 1. The client cannot choose which fan represents which area of life. The cards in this reading are always read in the following order:

Fan 1: what can be gained
Fan 2: what can be lost
Fan 3: what can be achieved
Fan 4: what can be lost

Read the cards in four groups of 3 in each fan. Every third card is used as the last card of the group you read next. There will be a discrepancy when you reach the fourth group of cards in the fan, as there will be a card missing. In this case, use card number 6 as the first card of the batch, card number 7 as the second, and card number 8 as the third. See Figure 4 for clarification. Repeat this method for all 4 fans.

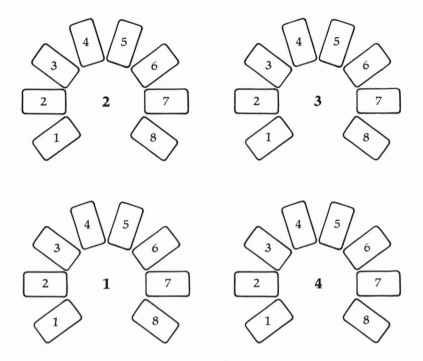

Figure 5. The Four Fans. This reading is done using a 32 card deck.

THE FOUR JACKS

This is a method in which the 4 jacks play a central role representing the twelve months in the year. Remove them from the deck and place them on a table as shown in Figure 6 on page 26. The jack of clubs will be Position 1, the jack of hearts in position 2, the jack of spades in position 3, and the jack of diamonds in position 4. The jacks are always set up in these positions, no matter when during the year you are doing this reading. This is the kind of reading you would do when a client wants to know the timing of specific events, of if something planned can be done at the client's convenience.

Take the remaining cards (28 cards should be left in the deck) and have the client shuffle them. Do not cut the deck. Lay

6 cards around the jack of clubs in the order indicated in Figure 6. The seventh card is placed on top of the jack of clubs, and this card indicates the final decision. Repeat the same process for the jack of hearts, spades and diamonds.

To interpret this reading, keep in mind what question you are to answer. Each jack rules a particular season as listed below:

> Position 1—Jack of Clubs—January, February, and March
> Position 2—Jack of Hearts—April, May, and June
> Position 3—Jack of Spades—July, August, and September
> Position 4—Jack of Diamonds—October, November, and December

If your client wants to know what is happening now, read the position for the current month first. If the client wants to know what will happen in the fall, go to the position that rules the season that is of concern.

In order to read the cards for a particular position, we'll use position 1 as an example. It is ruled by the jack of clubs. To start, we investigate two sets of 3 cards: cards 1, 2, and 3 for the jack of clubs; then cards 4, 5, and 6 for the same jack. The second card in each group, or card 2 and 5 in Figure 6, are the links between the other two. After determining what is symbolized by the cards as they are laid out, you can consider the whole section for the jacks of clubs, looking at all the cards in the sequence in which they were laid out. In other words, look at card 1 and see how it relates to card 2; then look at how card 2 relates to card 3; and how card 3 relates to card 4. At the end of the sequence, you have a final decision that is symbolized by card 7. This is the card that symbolizes the outcome of the whole situation.

The 7 cards can also be interpreted to represent the different days of the week.

> Card 1 = Sunday
> Card 2 = Monday
> Card 3 = Tuesday
> Card 4 = Wednesday
> Card 5 = Thursday
> Card 6 = Friday
> Card 7 = Saturday

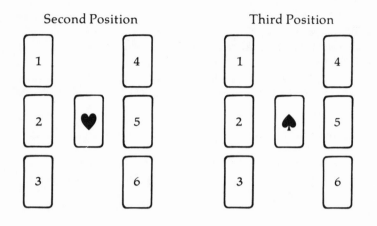

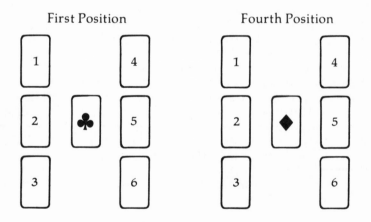

Figure 6. The Four Jacks. The cards are laid out according to the four jacks and the four seasons. The seventh card in each position will be placed over the jack for that position.

This is true of the cards in all four positions in Figure 6. This method can be especially useful if you want to get a sense of a particular day—a birthday, perhaps—or some other day of equal significance.

You should pay attention to the presence of picture cards in the position representing a birth month. If money cards are found, wealth is indicated. If the nine or ten of hearts occurs in this group, happiness and unexpected good luck are likely to enter the client's life.

This particular layout can be read another way, if you are interested in predicting a small or seemingly insignificant event which might otherwise be missed using the techniques outlined above. Pair card 1 with card 4; then pair card 2 with card 5; then card 3 with card 6. Leave card 7 until the very end and read card 7 from position 1 with card 7 from position 2 to see what will result. Then read card 7 from position 3 with card 7 from position 4 and see what result comes from there. Again, in order to read the cards this way, you will have to start with the position (or the jack) that rules the time of your question.

THE HALF MOON

This method is used when you don't know exactly why you are doing the reading. If someone just wants to have a reading done, but has no specific questions to ask you, this would be a good reading to do. The Half Moon is primarily a reading that is done when a short time span is being covered. Many readers use this reading at parties where there are many young people, or when doing a reading for someone who is very apprehensive about the cards.

The deck of 32 cards is used. First the client shuffles the cards. Then you hold the cards in your hands, face down, but spread open so that the client may pick nine cards. The first card is placed on the table face down. The second card is placed next to it, but in the shape of a half-moon. Start from the left and work in a semi-circle. When the first nine cards are placed, ask the client to draw nine more cards, face down, from the cards you hold in your hands. The second batch of nine cards is laid on top of the first with the first card in the second batch being placed on top of the first card from the first batch. You end up with nine positions in a half-moon configuration, with each of the nine positions having 2 cards. The cards are read in pairs, starting with the pair to the far left, and working in order to the right-hand side of the spread. Each position rules one area of the client's life, as follows:

Position 1: someone the client will meet
Position 2: someone the client will love
Position 3: someone who tires or wearies the client
Position 4: something which brings peace or comfort
Position 5: something hanging over the client's head
Position 6: something which helps the client
Position 7: something which surprises or astonishes the client
Position 8: something longed for
Position 9: something pleasant that will take place

Keep in mind that this is a short term reading, and whatever you discuss should be considered on a short range basis. This particular reading presents interesting information and the results of the reading take place shortly after the reading has been done.

THE GREAT STAR

The form of a star is often used for predicting with the cards. No matter what shape you use, or how many cards you use, it is essential that an uneven number of cards be drawn. Some readers use 13, 15, or 17 cards. The Great Star, which is explained here, uses 21 cards which are arranged around the personal card. This reading can be used for many different purposes, and you may wish to experiment with it to decide how it will work best for you.

Look at Figure 7 to see how the cards will be positioned. You will work with the deck of 32 cards, so the personal card will have to be located using the gypsy system. This means you select a king or a queen that best describes your client's features. If you are reading for a blond man, for example, you would choose the king of hearts to represent him.

Then give the deck (now 31 cards) to your client to shuffle. When he is done, have him cut the cards with his left hand. Ask him to cut the cards to the left, placing the right hand pile of

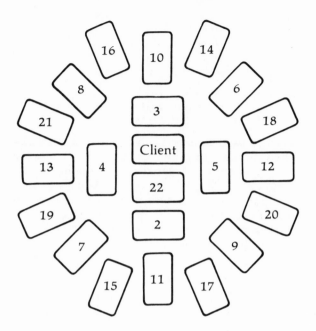

Figure 7. The Great Star. The client is symbolized by card number 1. All the rest of the cards are placed according to the positions shown here.

cards on the top of the other. You then take the top and bottom card away, placing the top card in position 2 and the bottom card in position 3. Ask him to cut the deck again, using the same procedure as before. You take the top and bottom cards away, placing the top card in position 4 and the bottom card in position 5. Continue on with this system until you have filled all the available positions in Figure 7.

The cards are read in pairs, beginning with the outside ring and moving to the inner ring. Work with the cards as follows:

Outside Ring: Cards 14 and 16
                    Cards 21 and 19
                    Cards 15 and 17
                    Cards 20 and 18

Inner Ring:	Cards 6 and 10
	Cards 9 and 12
	Cards 8 and 13
	Cards 7 and 11
Center Cards:	Cards 4 and 2
	Cards 5 and 3

The last card to be read is the one in position 22, which is read alone. When interpreting the cards, look at the pairs and compare each pair to the personal card symbolizing your client. You may find that the outer ring symbolizes outer circumstances, while the inner ring tells you more of what is going on within the client himself. You may notice different impressions in regard to this reading, and you should let your intuition guide you when using this spread.

THREE AND FOUR OF A KIND

When cards appear in a layout in pairs, it means that each card is increased in importance by the presence of the other. Should 3 or 4 cards of equal numerical value appear in a spread, each card has the meaning shown below.

4 Aces: Great strength and power; dynamic, radical changes.

3 Aces: Chances, motion, new interests, more success than was expected in an enterprise.

a) When the *ace of spades* is missing, it indicates much pleasure and new friends.
b) When the *ace of hearts* is missing, the changes have no connection with love or domestic affairs.
c) When the *ace of diamonds* is missing, the changes will have little connection with business or money.
d) When the *ace of clubs* is missing, the changes will have a negligible effect on the social life.

4 Kings: *For a male client*—new business connections, a growing circle of friends, praise, respect, great responsibility. *For a female client*—new relationships with men, the possibility of domestic or professional troubles and jealousy.

3 Kings: *For a male client*—new business contacts, pleasure in association with men. When 3 rather than 4 kings are together, there is less chance of unpleasant developments or the imposition of duties, and more prospects for amusement or success. *For a female client*—a larger circle of male friends, chances of business or romantic alliances, a greater sense of her own femininity. Where 3 rather than 4 kings appear, there is less chance of quarrels, jealousy and other unpleasant complications, and more prospect of lasting pleasure with new friends.

4 Queens: *For a male client*—a situation which can be shameful, ridiculous, even hazardous. He may become involved in jealous scenes and he will do well not to take himself too seriously. His sense of loyalty will cause a conflict of conscience, but his insight into the relativity of things can save him. *For a female client*—gossip. She must realize that her life-style is viewed with interest and perhaps some envy by other women or colleagues. It would be better if she would not take any unseemly interference in her affairs seriously, nor should she lose her sense of humor. If she takes gossip to heart, she may immobilize herself.

3 Queens: Meetings with prominent figures. Both male and female clients would do well to make a few new acquaintances among the women they meet in the near future. They will not regret it. A male client should not expect these women to reveal their deepest feelings to him on first meeting. Only by honest and warm responsiveness can he elicit the response he wants.

4 Jacks: Contacts with young people, a quick approach to unexpected situations.

3 Jacks: Correspondence, news of all kinds

> a) If the *jack of spades* is missing, the news will be exclusively good and cheerful.
> b) If the *jack of hearts* is missing, the news will bear no relation to love or family.
> c) If the *jack of diamonds* is missing, the news will not concern financial matters.
> d) If the *jack of clubs* is missing, the news will not encroach on any friendships.

4 Tens: Since tens represent entrances, it means that old paths in life are closed and new ones opened. Advise your client to

adapt a new life-style and make use of the opportunities it offers.

3 Tens: Signifies the same as 4 tens, but to a lesser extent.

> a) If the *ten of spades* is missing, the loss of old friends or familiar habits will cause no sorrow.
> b) If the *ten of hearts* is missing, no radical changes will take place at home or in the family.
> c) If the *ten of diamonds* is missing, there will be no fundamental changes in business or financial situations.
> d) If the *ten of clubs* is missing, changes will not bring loss of friends or social activities.

4 Nines: Fulfillment of long-cherished dreams and expectations, but with the proviso that the fulfillment may not bring the joy desired. The client should prepare for unexpected disappointment.

3 Nines: Happiness from an unexpected quarter; wishes fulfilled. It may seem as though a whim of fate brings unhappiness, but the contrary will be true.

4 Eights: Equilibrium and adaptation in daily life; tranquil joy; a combination of material comfort and spiritual insight.

3 Eights: Heightened capacity to handle difficulties and to enjoy more of life; strengthened character; inner happiness; ability to cope with strokes of good luck or setbacks; uniformity.

4 Sevens: Danger of conflicts, quarrels, disappointments; control, courage and duty are urgently needed.

3 Sevens: Faultfinding, chattering, chance of false accusations. When 3 sevens are found in a layout, the client should not be dissuaded from lofty plans, and should be urged to ignore any jealousy or unfairness directed from another. Adherence to principles may bear fruit.

4 Sixes: Slow progress on the path towards a goal. The client may be put to the test, but at the same time these cards warn against impatience.

3 Sixes: Hidden chances. It looks as though the client has a moment's respite and if the right attitude to personal affairs is taken, efforts will be rewarded by friendship, improvement in position, etc.

4 Fives: Orderliness, attention to detail, strict adherence to precepts. The client will continue to be deprived of joy in life if incapable of changing self-defeating habits or seeking new points of view.

3 Fives: Resistance to authority. Rash judgement may result in loss of prestige and waste of energy. Before taking action, the client would do well to determine whether aims are meaningful and have any chance of success.

4 Fours: Peace, quiet, immutability. This implies that life can offer little that is startling, but the client can continue to find satisfaction in the daily course of events.

3 Fours: Hardship. Relaxation after a struggle, illness or setback, a philosophical acceptance of limitation that can result in joy and peace of mind.

4 Threes: Dissatisfaction, new approaches and decisions. The client must take care not to be discouraged and you may want to point out that the future has to be built stone by stone and with the greatest possible attention to detail. The client must also learn to draw on new information.

3 Threes: Wrong conclusions, disappointments and discouragement. The client should be on guard against self-destructive tendencies and should be urged to turn everything known into concrete plans.

4 Twos: A period of trivialities, trifling presents, brief visits and stagnation, but pleasure in reading, art, hobbies and nature.

3 Twos: The same as 4 twos, with the following differences:

> a) If the *two of spades* is missing, troubles will be of minor importance. The days will be filled with small pleasures.
> b) If the *two of hearts* is missing, the pleasure will be found away from home, probably in chance meetings with strangers and in unexpected kindnesses on the part of superficial acquaintances.
> c) If the *two of diamonds* is missing, pleasure will be found in abstraction.
> d) If the *two of clubs* is missing, the pleasure will come from inner developments, heightened sensitivity to greater spiritual insight, peace of mind, or from a revived interest in neglected activities.

PREDOMINANCE OF ONE SUIT IN A LAYOUT

If a particular suit is clearly dominant in a layout, it gives the whole interpretation another emphasis. This happens, for example, if one is reading with 15 cards and one suit is represented by 5 or more cards. Since the picture cards are often used as personal cards, this change is of lesser significance unless there are 3 or 4 of them present.

A predominance of *spades* indicates unexpected events. It implies a suggestion of motion, disturbed plans, confusion and change. In general, spades mean disappointment and powers at work outside the client's control. They should not be interpreted as accidents and failure. Throughout the ages, spades have been cards of mystery, pointing the way to the unknown. They signify a challenge which the client may be able to use to advantage.

A predominance of *hearts* means joy, conviviality, pleasure and amusement. In addition, hearts can be viewed as cards of security, tenacity, good health and frivolity. Too many hearts in a spread may denote idleness, love of ease, self-indulgence and lack of concern for the welfare of others. Hearts generally suggest the need for a choice between the tranquil joys of contemplation, insight and compassion on the one hand and the more stimulating, but temporary pleasures of sensuality on the other.

A predominance of *diamonds* indicate money, business, success and respect. Diamonds combined with unfavorable spades could indicate a bad end to financial plans. This could be a result of lawsuits, the unexpected loss of financial resources through illness, or plans which have been thwarted through a misuse of trust, setbacks, or world crises. On the other hand, a combination of diamonds and hearts indicates that plans will run smoothly and that a goal will be easily attained. When more than 5 diamonds are present in a layout, the client should be warned against being too materialistic and should pay more attention to other aspects of life.

A predominance of *clubs* signifies a varied, more interesting life in the future. Clubs are generally cards of energy, enterprise, social orientation and practicality. They indicate the possibility of new relationships, a larger social life, and more spiritual activities. There is, however, a danger of making so many plans that none get off the ground. The client should be advised to limit activities until valuable friendships can be cultivated or ambitions which are closest to the heart are realized.

HIGH AND LOW CARDS IN THE LAYOUT

The presence of a large number of aces and picture cards in a spread indicates radical changes in life. This is certainly the case when nines or tens appear among the remaining cards. The presence of several high cards in a layout strengthens the influence of each card. They portend important events and indicate that the client will become closely involved with others, even taking part in activities which could not be managed alone.

If the layout consists mainly of low cards, it means that the client's life will undergo few noteworthy changes. Such a layout signifies that the cards only possess a rudimentary significance. For example: the promise of a letter with good news will be merely a pleasant experience, or quarrels will be nothing more than temporary dissatisfactions.

THE PICTURE CARDS

Picture cards often portray existing people. Since no two people are identical and a pack of cards has only a small number of picture cards, such a card cannot possibly give a complete picture of the person concerned. Some qualities will be lacking while others may not tally.

If you intend to give a detailed picture of such people, you must ask the client to shuffle the remaining cards once again. The client then draws 1 or 2 cards which you then place on the picture cards. These cards will furnish further information concerning the person characterized by the picture card.

Example 1: If the picture card is the queen of hearts and the card drawn is a three of diamonds, the woman indicated will be less naive than she seems, more cunning in financial matters and will tend to bargain.

Example 2: If the jack of diamonds is covered by the king of spades it means that the jack is no longer the adolescent he seems, but is well on the way to adulthood. To a certain extent he has already developed the stability and trustworthiness of the king of spades.

Example 3: If the queen of spades is covered by the nine of hearts, this combination means that the woman under discussion is lighthearted, cheerful, and even frivolous. It also means that her attitude to the client is of an intimate nature and that when she has the chance, she will help him to attain his goal.

THE JOKER

The joker comes from the fool in the tarot deck. It symbolizes someone who overthrows conventional attitudes as well as an independent spirit who goes his own way. The joker is self-sufficient, fearless, and instinctive in his wisdom. While on the material plane this card evokes an image of a muddle-headed person who is capable of all kinds of irresponsible mischief, mentally it symbolizes one who is original, witty, and imaginative.

Special Significance

If the joker appears in the middle of a layout, it signifies that the client is in the process of becoming free of physical shackles, and is driven by an unshakeable urge toward wholeness. No longer a slave to convention, this person has thrown off unnecessary banality, fear and desire and consequently acts with a united mind and spirit. This unity, however, is only experienced in rare cases. The presence of the joker does not mean that the unity is an accomplished fact. The card can help your client recognize marvellous inner powers and stimulate a desire to build life in accordance with those powers. This card will not prevent anyone from feeling hindered by everyday life and obligations. The nature of these obligations will be apparent from the cards which surround the joker.

If the joker lies in the left-hand corner of the spread, it indicates the client will have to choose between two possibilities: rejecting daily grind in order to gain freedom, or accepting material limitations in order to meet social responsibilities. In the bottom corner, the joker is associated with situations in which the client will either be able to act in accordance with ideals or will compromise them in order to gain personal advantage.

The joker always suggests that everything is not what it appears to be. A hidden meaning lies behind the overt significance of the cards. Wherever the joker appears, you (as the reader) should be very careful of your interpretation of the combination. Refrain from a too literal explanation of the cards, because in so doing, you may misread them. The joker is a card with many faces. It often clothes the future in riddles.

PART II
THE SUITS AND
THE NUMBERS

INTRODUCTION

Part II is an overview of the four suits in the deck, followed by a general breakdown of the numbers and what they signify. Part III will take each card in each suit and discuss its positive and negative (or reversed) meanings. Before moving to a specific discussion about the cards, it is important to understand the basic premise that lies behind both the suits and the numbered cards within the suits.

Each suit describes a special kind of person. When a person has a lot of clubs or diamonds in a spread, for example, it indicates a particular kind of activity, energy, or personality. Different suits represent different seasons in the year, and understanding each suit will help you become a better reader.

The numbers have a particular meaning as well, for you will notice that all twos relate in some way to pairs of opposites, while all fours have some tie to the concept of security. Even the picture cards have a numerical meaning, and that symbolism can be related to the reading.

In order to be the most effective card reader you can be, this section needs to be committed to memory so that you will automatically sense the meaning of the suits and numbers discussed here. By thoroughly understanding the underlying principles, you may even intuitively learn more about what the card means to you, as each reader develops a highly individualized interpretation for the cards.

THE SUITS

CLUBS ♣

Intuition, Sensitivity, Spontaneity

Positive: warmth, honesty, willpower, inspiration, creativity, intuition, self-confidence, independence, love of liberty, inventiveness

Negative: impatient, reckless, arrogant, condemning, melodramatic, uncommunicative, self-indulgent, vain, pompous, overbearing, chaotic

People who are symbolized by clubs face the world with spontaneity, great warmth and trust. They are energetic, enthusiastic and have a powerful, inspiring effect on their surroundings. Their spontaneity and self-confidence grows out of a need to express creativity, and thus result in a lack of patience and tact. They are ambitious about the pursuit of goals and anything which stands in the way is dispensed with accordingly. "On to new possibilities, the past is history," could be the motto of clubs.

Clubs attract other people like magnets, and in the process, gather a large circle of friends around them. If things do not go as they wish or expect—and that does indeed occasionally happen—they react explosively and angrily. However, their anger is as brief as it is intense and they are not ones to hold grudges. Clubs are also irascible, tyrannical, obtrusive, and arrogant. They are given to melodramatic displays and consider themselves God's gift to the world.

Clubs represent the spring, childhood, youth, a child's first relationships with family and friends, the first love affair, the reproductive urge, the inclination towards self-sacrifice for friends, fatherland or convictions. Clubs also have a need for luxury and comfort, gaiety and pleasure. Professionally they can be found in occupations where creativity is useful and routine or repetition is not the order of the day.

In sum, clubs are trustworthy, independent, energetic and spontaneous. They are filled with an unceasing impulse to seize every opportunity which comes their way and explore it in depth.

HEARTS ♥

Love, Self-sacrifice, Service

Positive: a stimulating force in any group, a loyal and self-sacrificial person, a truth-seeker

Negative: materialistic, greedy, grasping, scheming, emotionally blackmailing, overly sentimental, lethargic, energy-draining, chaotic

Nothing is as important to a hearts type of person as feelings and relationships. Without them existence would be infertile and without hope. Everything is sacrificed for relationships and it is typical of hearts to cause a crisis, even at great personal cost, with the aim of eliciting a response, any response, from a partner.

The emotional world in all its variety is the breath of life for hearts. It is a world which is continuous, ever-changing and fluid, and where differences have little meaning. The only distinction that hearts make is whether or not something feels good, although establishing this difference does not imply condemnation. The inner life of the hearts person lies so close to the archaic roots of existence that personal standards may remain unconscious. Hearts react, nothing more, but these instinctive reactions are almost always right and accurate. The hearts' motto could be, "The left hand does not know what the right is doing."

Hearts describe people who are friendly, sympathetic characters, susceptible to outside impressions, and who are fairly pliable. Conviviality is a primary requirement for hearts and they are particularly hospitable people. Their most striking characteristics are sympathy, compassion, care and protection, and they can always put others at ease. They are indefatigable searchers after the truth and have a strength and perserverance in this respect, which not only elicits admiration, but in the long run, wins over every kind of oppostion. The obstacles encountered in life bring hearts pain, grief and loss. The path taken is definitely not an easy one and they are often forced to sacrifice personal wishes, motives and love in the service of it.

Hearts represent the summer, adulthood and growth. Professionally, work may be concerned with giving care, protection and assistance to others. Hearts may be doctors, nurses, custodians, or welfare workers in rehabilitation centers or in institutions fighting against such things as alcoholism and the misuse of drugs. They are also commonly found in positions such as curators, guardians and executors of wills.

The unsympathetic aspects of their character may be expressed by a possessive, oppressive attachment to others, emotional fanaticism, anxiety, or a dark stifling attitude which makes every relationship seem like a scene from Othello. They are given to exaggerated expressions of sentimentality, get lost in romantic daydreams, and are plagued by irresolution. Hearts often show signs of melancholy and suffer from a lack of vitality.

In sum, hearts need to mother, protect and to keep everyone they care for near them. As friendly and romantic as they may be, hearts are often quick to take offense. Their fear and sorrow in this respect may be expressed as timidity and suspicion. As soon as they really feel that things are safe again, free rein is given to sensitivity, sympathy and compassion.

SPADES ♠

Knowledge, Desire for Knowledge, Aloofness

Positive: energetic, brilliant, cheerful, vital, humorous, easy-going, communicative, well-informed, independent, sober, aloof, self-possessed

Negative: uncertain, fickle, sensational, gossiping, superficial, inaccurate, slovenly, careless, melancholy, pessimistic, lifeless and cynical

Spades represent that aspect which distinguishes man from beast—thought. They also symbolize autumn and middle-age. Of the four suits, spades are the furthest removed from the instinctive, primitive powers which lie at the root of life. Through differentiation, analysis, and objectivity, spades can create sufficient distance to ensure effective action in emotional situations.

Spades excel in analysis; they collect and catalogue information. Spades are not only endowed with a sharp intelligence, but are able to view situations objectively. They have a precise sense of justice and an inborn understanding of human weakness. Their capacity for logical and systematic thought does not keep them from displaying a preference for culture, art and beauty. The flexibility of mind and ability to absorb new ideas is sometimes misinterpreted by others as opportunism.

Spades, however, have a problem with the realm of emotions. Feelings do not lend themselves to analysis, and when faced with situations which cannot be intellectualized, spades often find themselves adrift. They are not without the resources to see the psychological underpinnings of emotional behavior and this does make for some balance.

Spades frequently apply their intelligence to their own ventures and to the activities of those endowed with a less lucid mind. They investigate, analyze, teach, spread news and propagandize. Professionally, we frequently find spades in education, journalism, advertising, and in all fields of communications and information-dispersal. Many writers, publishers, radio and television assistants are spades.

Spades can be vacillating, fickle, superficial figures who skip from one subject to another without pausing to learn one in depth. They excel in the use of a sharp, aggressive tongue. Some can be sly and unreliable and deserving of the charge of dishonesty.

In sum, spades are excitable, tense, intellectually gifted people who are capable of holding their own in any conversation. In general, liveliness and lightheartedness leads them to walk cheerfully through life, never losing their sense of humor. They are not without close relationships because righteousness attracts many emotionally giving people.

DIAMONDS ◆

Possessions, Financial Affairs, the Spirit of Enterprise

Positive: practical, solid, persevering, industrious, patient, genuine, sober, determined, goal-oriented, modest, quiet, obliging, tolerant, acquiescent, sensual

Negative: cringing, pitiless, willful, fussy, fault-finding, critical, selfish to the point where the end justifies the means

Diamonds represent people's tendency to rely solely on the evidence of the senses. They are best described as the "reality principle." Diamonds are able to make order out of sense impressions and build an enormous collection of factual knowledge, which renders them capable of acting efficiently in any situation. The motto of diamonds should be, "It is visible, tangible, audible and palpable; therefore it exists."

Diamonds are trustworthy, enterprising, tenacious people who go about their business in a levelheaded and efficient manner. They work at building up possessions until a sense of well-being is achieved. From this they derive a sense of values, which is essential, since they stand or fall on the basis of values. Diamonds are in their element in the material world and can handle money and take responsibility superbly. They are sensual, feel at home with their bodies and usually enjoy good health since they pay attention to physical needs.

Diamonds represent winter, old age, sustenance and prosperity. They are patient and forgiving, have great self-discipline and indefatigable energy. In the career area, they are often found as the trustworthy, driving force behind a business. This usually means they are administrators. In addition, diamonds have a flair for organization and a business instinct which leads to success. We also find them in mining, international trade, industrial enterprise, stockbroking and banking.

In the negative sense, they can be narrow-minded, dogmatic and extremely possessive of property. Diamonds can and will ignore the more subtle emotional experiences of life, as these are not concrete and are therefore considered absurd. They have an inclination to melancholy, are sometimes frankly pessimistic, and often lack the ability to be spontaneous.

In sum, although diamonds excel in collecting facts, they frequently miss the significance in the relationship between these facts as well as the motivation behind them. While diamonds play at controlling the material world, the inner significance of the personal life may elude them because sensory perception is not a substitute for thought.

THE NUMBERS

THE ACES

Endeavoring, Ruling, Wanting, Independent

The aces represent individuality, independence, and leadership. People described by aces are particularly difficult to keep in check. Explosive desires will occasionally cause them to meet with opposition, but the willful aces do not allow themselves to be diverted. They don't change their minds, they remain true to their own uniqueness. In order to do so they are willing to violate prevailing codes, laws and precepts. Less powerful figures will often come to ask for support and advice which will be generously given. Interchange with others is also essential but it occurs on the ace's terms. Aces consider themselves masters of their own homes and wish to remain so.

Clubs: desire for spontaneity
Diamonds: desire for possessions
Spades: desire for knowledge
Hearts: desire for love

THE TWOS

Being Together, Going Together, Working Together

The twos represent all pairs of opposites—male and female, light and dark, hot and cold, wet and dry, action and reaction. In practice, this boils down to the fact that the person represented by the two is in search of his or her other half. This frequently manifests as a fear of being alone and an unceasing search for support and completion through another. Acting in multiples of two is a defense against uncertainty and fear. It follows then, that twos are very sensitive to outside opinion and are at their best in an environment which is receptive. Other people are essential for twos of all suits, and the cards surrounding them will indicate environmental influences. The transmission of messages and news is ascribed to them since they hear and see much.

Clubs: the search for freedom and spontaneity in being together.
Diamonds: the search for profitable partnerships
Spades: the search for people with like minds
Hearts: the search for unity through love

THE THREES

Uncertainty, Personal Development

The people represented by three suffer from indecisiveness because they cannot distinguish between what is and what is not attainable. They waste time, energy, and especially words (their great strength) because they never head directly for a goal, but wander irresolutely and confusedly in other directions. They are willing, and certainly try to keep to their original intention, but situations often arise and demand a decision which causes them to panic. Due to their eloquence and capacity for contact, they have many friends and acquaintances who bail them out at precisely the right moment. Their flexible, responsive character enables them to extricate themselves from almost any difficult situation and to turn it to their benefit. Any door can be opened with well-placed words. They certainly use words, but often too profusely. The threes possess considerable energy which enables them to recover quickly from shocks and disappointments.

> *Clubs:* uncertainty about the nature of their relationships
> *Diamonds:* uncertainty about their decisions with respect to property
> *Spades:* uncertainty about the value of their ideas
> *Hearts:* uncertainty about their choice of partner

THE FOURS

Structure and Building

The fours represent security and protection. People who are described by these cards build a solid foundation for themselves and their families. Through hard work and concentration they are able to live life the way they want, overcoming obstacles such as poverty, sorrow and failure. The fours are among the most favorable cards. They indicate a good basis for security and prosperity, but the neighboring cards in the spread will describe how this will be used. The fours are a mixture of mind and matter, and anyone who attempts to split these constituents is building his security on quicksand and can count on a lonely, melancholy old age. The fours enjoy building. They are equal to almost any situation and they feel gloriously at home when in the thick of things. They have the capacity and patience to build the future slowly, and in doing so, to purchase everything which money can buy. The fours are able to obtain tangible results through practical knowledge; they do whatever is necessary and are not afraid to soil their hands. This is fortunate since success does not usually come easily. Adherence to moral and social laws provide them with the needed structure to accomplish goals.

Clubs: structures based on insight into the value of their relationships
Diamonds: structures based on the development of a personal value system
Spades: structures based on the acquisition of special knowledge
Hearts: structures based on love

THE FIVES

Discord, Restlessness, Change

The fives represent discord. People who are depicted by these cards suffer from an almost compulsive restlessness and change homes, loves, jobs, environment, friends and clothes with equal frequency. As soon as one change is complete, they have already started on the next, because there is always the possibility that somethings lies beyond the next horizon. Freedom is emblazoned in gold letters on their coat of arms. Concentration does not come easily to the fives: they strongly resemble the knight in the fairytale who mounted his horse and rode off in all directions. These changes do result in a considerable knowledge of human nature. This does not in any way alter the fives' innate honesty and sense of justice. What could be greater evidence of their strength? It is this same strength which allows them to keep moving and forces them to search harder and further, and it is the search itself which provides their greatest satisfaction in life.

It is not uncommon for fives to find they are the center of interest, and this position is used to push on even further in the pursuit of knowledge and change. Experience, rather than performance, drives them. They are not career-seekers. When negatively expressed, the five can manifest as one who hates the environment, other people, even life itself. They refuse to accept any responsibility for this whatsoever. They may act as if their freedom is constantly under attack. When this happens, they are not too trustworthy. The innate, objective sense of justice is not expressed very well if freedom is threatened. The most important thing in life is personal growth, and if the five is negative, this may be pursued at the expense of others.

If the external changes which affect the fives are in accordance with their stage of development, they generally have a positive influence. If their restlessness is, on the other hand, caused by discord, then instead of the equilibrium and tranquility which the fives so desperately seek, chaos and panic set in. The fives live life in a sensual and intense way. They will extract what is best from every situation, but holding on to people and things past their limited usefulness causes frustration. They tend to go hunting after pleasure and usually satisfy this urge. Love affairs will play a major role and may be numerous, very intense, but of short duration. The innate versatility and ingenuity of the fives leads them to take on several things at the same time. A job will seldom ever be finished because a thirst for adventure will always be urging them onward.

> *Clubs:* problems with cutting the bonds of friendship when necessary
> *Diamonds:* problems with differences of opinion in business
> *Spades:* problems with shifting viewpoints
> *Hearts:* problems with breaking unhealthy emotional alliances

THE SIXES

Mediation, Adaptation, Understanding of Life

The sixes have a very special place in life. They signify people who are driven by a sense of mission, purpose, and calling. The Pythagoreans called the number six the perfect number, fully symmetrical, the form of forms. In daily life, they represent beauty, harmony, order, perfection and the family with its cares and responsibilities. Numerically the sixes symbolize the archetypal parent, the guardian and comforter, the educator and guide, the protector and provider of shelter. They stand for unity and working together, for adaptation and responsibility.

Their path in life is definitely not a bed of roses, because a sense of duty in relation to others often stands in the way of personal desires and aims. The bustling sixes find it particularly difficult to adjust to inactivity and passivity. In general, they feel responsible for the welfare of the environment in which they live. They are bearers of other people's troubles and comforters and peacemakers by nature. Where necessary they will always lend help and assistance to the family and the community. Maladjusted people who find it difficult to stand on their own two feet will come to them for assistance.

Since the sixes shoulder many burdens and let the welfare of others take precedence, it is important to mention here that too much sacrifice can disturb emotional equilibrium. They should be prepared to accept the same benevolence from others which they give to the world. When difficulties arise, the sixes usually have a guardian angel standing in the wings. From the negative point of view, the six represents postponement and living in a rut, an aversion to growth and advance, and a resistance to activity. Instead of listening to the inner life, they ruthlessly work for personal advancement and may ignore the needs of others.

> *Clubs:* trusting their own insight in order to attain stability
> *Diamonds:* accepting the consequences of their own deeds in order to learn responsibility
> *Spades:* sharing their knowledge with others in order to learn the free exchange of ideas
> *Hearts:* practicing benevolence in order to enlarge reality

THE SEVENS

Insight, a Turning Point

The sevens are difficult cards to understand because they are mainly spiritual in their import. They represent the need for self-reflection and the necessity for pausing to evaluate the life path. The sevens often indicate the turning points in life. People denoted by sevens strive for perfection, but never fully attain it because they usually fail to take the time for it. They don't always have the insight to subject the life situation to critical investigation. Sevens also have to cope with a lack of understanding from others in regard to personal life and vision. The sevens' striving, of itself, may cause others discomfort and dissatisfaction because a life which is lived from the deepest layers of being cannot but reveal the shortcomings in lives with less depth. Consequently, the sevens' circle of friends is small and marriage partners are not in abundance.

The sevens' aptitude for analysis and synthesis is extensive. Interests lie in the field of scientific research and a sharp intellect and profound intuition add extra depth to their work. The opportunity for education is usually available and should be seized with both hands. The sevens will often search for the hidden meanings of life. It is essential to understand that being alone is not the same as being lonely. Sevens feel most comfortable when alone and will frequently lead a solitary life. They will be most successful when life is allowed to take its course.

>*Clubs:* warning against rash plans and self-complacency
>
>*Diamonds:* warning against relying too much on their own judgment
>
>*Spades:* warning against overestimating the value of success
>
>*Hearts:* warning against a hostile expression of dissatisfaction in love relationships

THE EIGHTS

Power, Will, Organization

Eights are power cards. When an eight appears in the spread for someone who uses money as power, it usually has negative connotations, since such an attitude usually brings about its own ruin. Power can be applied to good ends or bad. Misuse of power occurs all too frequently in negative eights who consider themselves above the law. People who are denoted by eights are destined to circulate and work in well-to-do circles. They have great physical endurance and use their almost inexhaustible store of energy constructively and efficiently. In addition, they are good judges of people. They extract the utmost from every opportunity. Eights are born to lead. They are adept at surveying the people and situations around them. A word of warning should be given here (although it is not likely to be heeded). The client is advised to act respectfully when delegating work to others because only then can help be expected when it is needed. Without thinking very much about it, eights sweep aside all restrictions as a matter of course and reject any interference in their affairs. They are able to control situations because they sense the larger picture. They are self-sufficient.

> *Clubs:* can and will live according to ideals without losing sight of practicality
>
> *Diamonds:* can and will accumulate wealth without emphasizing material success
>
> *Spades:* can and will acquire knowledge without losing sight of sensual pleasures
>
> *Hearts:* can and will live a well-balanced life without being on guard against emotional invasions from outside

THE NINES

Desire, the Grand Passion, Philanthropy

The nines contain the combined energy of all the preceeding cards. They are all-embracing, powerful and forward-looking. They signal both endings and beginnings. They are often seen, on superficial examination, as the cards of disappointment, but they in fact signify the striving for fulfillment. The power of people described by the nines is difficult to channel or contain within the limitations of the material world. They love more violently than others and their surrender is more impassioned because they draw directly from the primeval source of life. They recognize few personal ties and do not engage in long-term alliances.

Nines are more idealistic than others, but in view of their nature they are disillusioned more easily, and therefore suffer more than the rest of us. The nines imply great desires and grand passions, but personal desires or love affairs usually cause difficulties, frustrations, sorrow and loss. They may be inspiring to others but may not be successful in dealing on a mundane, day-to-day basis with relationships. Nines help, mediate, instruct, are entertaining and hospitable. They are able to win others over to their viewpoint through the strength of their convictions. They are by nature sympathetic and possess insight which enables them to take a generous attitude toward others. The best chances for the nines lie in generously giving of themselves without expecting anything in return. But herein lies the greatest risk, for this is a dangerous path along the razor's edge of existence. Those who tread this path either sink or swim.

> *Clubs:* the longing to be one with the universe; disappointment through ego-oriented goals
>
> *Diamonds:* the longing for the riches of nature; disappointment through a narrow focus on personal prosperity
>
> *Spades:* the longing for insight into universal laws; disappointment through the use of knowledge for personal glory
>
> *Hearts:* the longing for love; disappointment when the willingness to serve is limited to a small circle

THE TENS

Success, Completion

The tens are called success cards, a term which can sound rather weak and imprecise. The nines represent the completion of a cycle of human experience. A new one begins at the ten on a higher level: the cycle of human endeavor. Since success is a purely personal question, we find in the tens a wide variety of expression. Whatever goal they pursue, they are excellently equipped to attain it.

> *Clubs:* success after the application of ideals to practice
>
> *Diamonds:* success in possessions amassed with dedication and care
>
> *Spades:* success following intellectual cooperation with others
>
> *Hearts:* success through the overcoming of obstacles by love

THE JACKS

Idealism, Youth, the Messenger

The jacks represent youth and signify people who are mobile, neutral, and matter-of-fact. They are distinguished by an intelligent attitude to life. Since experience is the best schoolmaster of all for them, they are always on the lookout for new adventures. They can best be characterized as "inspired receivers" and from a mythological point of view they most resemble the messenger of the gods, Mercury. From a temporal point of view, they make good errand boys, postmen, or inspectors. They are always able to use their intelligence in the service of a practical goal. Jacks traditionally represent a son or a (young) friend. They often betray the hidden thoughts of the kings and queens of the same suit. Professionally they may be employed as travelling salesmen, journalists, and advertising personnel.

Negatively seen, jacks fritter away energy. They browse through life but never commit themselves to anything. They are often seen as neutral, undecided, frivolous people who are unable to make decisions or hold fast to a direction. They use their diplomacy as a defensive measure, although there is a certain stubbornness and tenacity in them. If this is a result of principles, so much the better, but this tendency is more often than not an expression of the youngster's conviction that he knows everything and is always right.

> *Clubs:* attain their goal through insight into the coherence of things
>
> *Diamonds:* attain their goal by sound financial management
>
> *Spades:* attain their goal by using exactly the right word at the right moment
>
> *Hearts:* attain their goal through sacrifice for the sake of love

THE QUEENS

Reacting, Judging

Each of the four queens represents, in her own way, the receptive, reproductive principle of life. They stand for the different images of women in all our lives. They bring to mind various mother goddesses such as Hera—the wife of the sungod; Demeter—the goddess of fertility; Pallas Athena—the virgin goddess of wisdom; and Aphrodite—the goddess of love and desire. Each of these mythological figures represents a specific psychic function: intuition, sensation, thought, and feeling. Each queen can be seen as a ruler and mediator of these realms of being.

Queens represent the receiving, cooperating part of the man-woman duality. In contrast with the kings, who are illustrated bearing swords, battle-axes or spears, the women are furnished with symbols of fertility, growth and blossoming. The queens react to external impulses. They judge them and then, based on that judgment, cherish or reject them. Hence it follows that the queens are by nature good lawyers, mediators and justices of the peace. In fortune-telling, queens were generally used as personal cards. Traditionally, the queen of diamonds stood for women with grey, red or sandy hair, and sometimes for widows who were very pale. Clubs designated women who were neither blond nor brunette. Hearts meant women with fair skin, brown hair, blue or grey eyes. Spades represented women who were very dark and who had black or dark brown hair and brown eyes.

Clubs: react, judge and rule through instinct
Diamonds: react, judge and rule over the amassing of property
Spades: react, judge, and rule over words and images
Hearts: react, judge and rule over desires and feelings

THE KINGS

Vitality, Authority

Each of the four kings represents, in his own way, the outgoing, energizing principle of life. Each stands for a different image of men in our lives. The kings bring to mind the different male gods in mythology, such as Zeus (Jupiter)—the sun god; Kronos (Saturn)—the god of time; Apollo—the god of eloquence and fine arts; and Dionysos—the god of intoxication. These mythological figures each represent a specific psychic function: instinct, intangibility, thought and feeling. Each of the kings can be viewed as the ruler of one of these realms. They represent the positive, activating, aggressive, outgoing part of the man-woman duality, both parts having equal value. It should be emphasized that the aggression of the kings is a function of initiative and action, rather than violence. These cards represent the founders and cornerstones of society, and those who realize men's ideals.

The authority of the kings seldom leads to tyranny, since they are generally understanding, sympathetic, friendly people who can see that power is dependent on cooperation. Indeed, in practice they are shown to their best advantage in partnerships. In fortune-telling, the kings represent a husband, father or older brother. If they are lying upside down in a spread, they indicate antagonistic, quarrelsome, aggressive behavior. Diamonds traditionally represent men with grey, red or sandy hair or widowers who look very pale. Clubs are chosen for men who are neither blond nor dark. Hearts signify men with pale skin, brown hair, blue or grey eyes. Spades indicate men who are very dark, and who have black or dark brown hair and brown eyes.

Clubs: use their authority to realize ideals
Diamonds: use their authority to acquire prosperity
Spades: use their authority to obtain knowledge
Hearts: use their authority mercifully for the maintenance of life

PART III
THE CARDS

INTRODUCTION

Part III is comprised of a listing of each of the fifty-two cards in the deck. We start with clubs, and move to hearts, spades and diamonds. Each card is interpreted on several different levels. First, the personal characteristics of each card are discussed. These apply to the person you are doing the reading for, and describe the characteristics and problems associated with the individual when the card is used as a personal significator. The second section under each card is a description of the card itself. For example, the two of clubs may be just one of many cards in a spread. What does it mean then? Each card changes when it is used as one of the cards in the reading, and this material is presented under its own heading.

The third heading is "Special Significance." When a card is surrounded by other cards, its value may change. For example, a five of clubs will operate differently when it is surrounded by diamonds or spades. Sometimes the value of a card will change if it appears in the middle of a spread, or in an upper or lower corner. If this is an issue, it has been mentioned in the third section. When no really important changes in the value of a card are based on position or on the surrounding cards, this third section has not been included.

Should you have further questions about the significance of a card, you may want to refer back to the suits and numbers as discussed in Part II, or the sections in Part I that pertain to the predominance of certain suits in a reading. High and low cards in a layout are also discussed in Part I.

Clubs

CLUBS: intuition, sensitivity, spontaneity

ACE: endeavoring, ruling, wanting, individuality

ACE OF CLUBS: high expectations, strong passions, "I want"

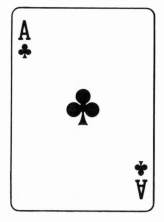

ACE OF CLUBS

Positive: power, directness, originality, creativity, talent, warmth, politeness, friendship, Spring

Negative: ambition, cunning, selfishness, provocation, chaos, violence, treachery, vacillation, dogmatism

Personal Characteristics

The ace of clubs represents a person who tends to be unsympathetic or indecisive when affection is shown by others. This individual has a different thought and action pattern than most other people, which sometimes causes conflicts with friends and acquaintances. The ace of clubs wants to be favorably regarded by friends and loved ones, yet also seeks peace and quiet, behaving in a very conservative and sometimes even dogmatic manner. Moods don't last long because this individual is basically broad-minded. Confusion arises when this individual tries to wield all the above mentioned characteristics at the same time, and by trying to keep on good terms with everyone, a great deal of inner pain may be experienced. The values which predominate will often depend on environment.

It is evident that such a person, chaotic and demanding on the one hand, philanthropic on the other, will want to be surrounded by affection and harmony. In the negative sense, the ace of clubs could also be vain, and altruism might stem from less disinterested motives than may seem apparent at first sight.

The Card

The ace of clubs is a card of talent. It indicates high expectations and ambition, energy and imagination, strong passions and the capacity to exchange feelings and thoughts with others. But we also learn from this card that not every promise is fulfilled and not every talent is used in the right way. Full development of creativity may be endangered by inner turmoil.

If the ace of clubs is centrally placed in a layout, it means that the client is richly endowed with artistic ability, strong intuition and explosive power. This person will have a lively imagination, also possessing the skill to pass on visions to the rest of us, either through the written word, pictorial art or music, or through a profession such as a minister, or other similar channels.

Some danger may be concealed in the ace of clubs: that of chaos. Too many talents in one person can end up destroying each other so none of the talents ever really develop. Acumen, powers of observation, and imagination serve no useful purpose if they cannot be channeled into a concrete mold.

The ace of clubs is generally distinguished by quick responses and therefore usually has no appreciation of the limitations of others. This card represents an artistic temperament which does not wish to be delayed by everyday banalities, a prophetic gift which reaches too high to be able to nourish a profound interest in earthly matters.

Tradition associates the ace of clubs with the nomad or tramp who restlessly follows the seasons and lives one day at a time. From a practical point of view, this means that the client with this card in a spread will enjoy a variety, sudden changes, or journeys. This person may also be unexpectedly seized by some form of beauty. The ace of clubs has no control at all over these emotions; they simply happen.

Special Significance

The reader's advice to the client should be guided by the cards surrounding the ace of clubs. If hearts dominate a spread the reader should caution the client against too great a love of pleasure, or against reaping the fruits of the day too intensely and too quickly since the client's talents can be easily wasted. If a spread is dominated by clubs, the propensity for human contact and a busy social life will delay, limit, or even prevent the development of artistic proficiency. A preponderance of diamonds signifies that the utilization and practice of dormant talent will produce financial rewards. Too many spades in a layout indicate that the client is too quickly discouraged by trifling setbacks. A balanced layout promises a more intensely lived life and increasing income from creative activity.

♣   ♣   ♣

CLUBS: intuition, sensitivity, spontaneity
TWO: being together, going together, working together
TWO OF CLUBS: spontaneously being together

TWO OF CLUBS

Positive: a harmonizing power who establishes rules of conduct and in so doing exercises influence over others. The two of clubs excels through self-confidence, gallantry and boldness.

Negative: rebellious, restless, tempestuous, may withdraw when challenged and refuse to yield to any viewpoint other than his own

Personal Characteristics

The two of clubs is very idealistic with regard to human relationships. This individual builds the most beautiful castles in the air but as usual, these castles have little in common with reality. Almost without exception the two feels too confident about specific relationships, and interferes in the most trifling matters, leaving others little or no freedom.

As a result of a profound interest in people, the two of clubs has a lively concern for the emotional underpinnings of their behavior. Unrealistic expectations concerning love, relationships and marriage frequently cause the most disappointment, because no mortal being can ever make this dream-world true. The conviction that people are not born to live alone makes the two run from one experimental relationship to another, from disappointment to disappointment, trying to avoid the idea of living alone. On the other hand, many alliances will leave this person in a state of confusion and disillusionment.

The two of clubs is strongly drawn to foreigners and/or foreign countries, and has a deep desire to maintain contact with people who live at a great distance. The love life plays as large a role in life as the desire for knowledge. Although the one may come into conflict with the other when emotions run too high, both the learning process and work come to a halt when everything goes wrong emotionally. When this is realized (usually too late) the individual may be overcome by remorse. This card is more self-critical and has more insight than the twos of other suits.

This person is intuitively aware that the cultivation of intelligence is part of destiny. But a two of clubs whose affairs of the heart take second place to the accumulation of knowledge may fare badly because of the feeling that the "best" in life has been missed. This could indicate a very melancholy person.

The Card

The two of clubs traditionally represents an invitation. This could be an introduction to a club, an invitation to a meeting, or a date for a meal. Although this invitation may seem trivial at first, the appearance of the two of clubs in a spread signifies that the acceptance of the invitation will have unexpected consequences for the client's life. This is especially true if the card is placed in the center of a spread.

Special Significance

Picture cards near the two of clubs indicate an invitation which will lead to new friendships. If such a picture card represents the opposite sex, and lies above or below the two of clubs, it contains the promise of a romance which will begin at a party. If the two of clubs appears in a layout where diamonds predominate, acceptance of the invitation will bring financial reward. If hearts predominate in a layout with the two of clubs, the invitation will smooth the way for many things the client has long desired.

The presence of other clubs indicates that convivial intercourse, merriment and parties will follow the acceptance of a chance invitation. If the ten of spades bars the way to the two of clubs, it indicates that acceptance of an invitation will have unpleasant consequences and that a refusal would be more advisable.

If the two of clubs lies in the center of a layout of a female client, it indicates she is convinced she can supply her partner with the characteristics which she believes he lacks. If the two of clubs lies in the center of a male client's combination, it signifies that he will be touchy, easily irritated and impatient although he will try with little success to hide it.

♣   ♣   ♣

CLUBS: intuition, sensitivity,
   spontaneity
THREE: uncertainty, personal
   development
THREE OF CLUBS: uncertainty
   caused by contacts

THREE OF CLUBS

Positive: innocent, childish, cheerful, curious, quick, contactual, a good conversationalist

Negative: cold, self-centered, stubborn, sensationalist, superficial, mischief-maker, dissident

Personal Characteristics

The three of clubs is a very social card and the person represented by this card may be completely ruled by the need to make social contacts. This underlying need can cause an appearance of a somewhat irresolute response to life. Interests lie mainly in the emotional alliances that are made, but they cause a certain amount of insecurity in the individual as this is an area of personality that requires the most growth. Upon entering an emotional relationship, you may observe the three of clubs being totally obsessed by it—even to the point of apparently drowning in a sea of emotion. Then the senses are regained for an instant and the three does a total about-face in order to keep the emotional chaos at a distance. It is difficult for the recipient of affection from the three of clubs to understand what has happened—as this card unwittingly causes others pain and sorrow. The situations may be repeated over and over.

This card needs to learn about action and behavior that hurts, even if the hurt to others is not intentional. The youthful owner of this card can hardly be reproached for the broken pieces of relationships left behind due to the innocence of youth. As the person matures, there is a tendency to rush from one extreme to the other. This is not so much inconsistency or disloyalty as it is an attempt to reconcile opposing impulses. The success of the attempt is another matter!

The three of clubs is quick and intelligent, and has a natural need for freedom, which may cause close relationships to become repugnant or tormenting, as freedom is impaired or the relationship becomes boring. A vague notion of standards, or the natural inclination to judge situations before they are fully understood, is another confusing trait.

It is widely believed that the three of clubs cannot distinguish between reality and fantasy, good and evil, or truth and falsehood. One often sees the indecisive, vacillating, three suddenly taken firmly in hand by a domineering figure who tries to restrain this individual by means of a leash. Natural resistance to domination may catapult the three into self-awareness and maturity—although the newly won maturity may not last for long. This card cannot stand limitations on freedom and may not remain in a stable relationship.

The Card

The three of clubs traditionally indicates an unpleasant period in someone's life during which social life can be hampered by disparaging treatment, expulsion or some kind of malicious insinuation. Since this does not have to end tragically, the appearance of this card in a combination is a warning to the client that any reaction to such treatment should not be so violent as to blow it out of proportion. It is better to scrupulously ensure that injured pride or irritated nerves do not lead to unseemly behavior, name-calling, or revenge. Should this occur, some retribution may take place. It would be most sensible for the client to take stock of the situation from a calm and philosophical point of view. The disparagement was perhaps not intended in the way that it was received, or the insinuation was not as serious as informers would have one believe. The surrounding cards should show how the incident could be advantageous to the client, if the situation is approached wisely.

Special Significance

Special care is recommended if hearts lie on one side of the three of clubs with spades on the other. A decisive choice must be made. Self-control and magnanimity will bring everything to a happy end. Anger and passion can cause such annoyance that it will endanger the future happiness of the client.

♣ ♣ ♣

CLUBS: intuition, sensitivity,
    spontaneity
FOUR: structure and building
FOUR OF CLUBS: tranquility
    through creative work

FOUR OF CLUBS

Positive: completeness, order, perfected work, fulfillment after great effort, peace, stability, acumen, subtlety. Learns from experience

Negative: unstable, unreliable due to excessive fear and worry, tendency to make hasty decisions that are wrong.

Personal Characteristics

Should financial problems occur, they will not cause the four of clubs much difficulty because an energetic approach usually causes them to disappear. This person needs money and the means to satisfy the need for money in a practical way. The four should make sure that a lust for money doesn't develop into greed.

The four of clubs has a bigger problem—learning how to handle the emotional sphere. Those who are cherished may not mature as quickly as the four of clubs. This individual walks to a different drummer, and may withdraw into a shell, living alone rather than communicating the personal nature to loved ones. If unable to induce loved ones to move voluntarily towards wider horizons, the four may opt for solitude since total satisfaction can be found in work.

The four of clubs uses knowledge well. This is an independent, introverted thinker, with a fixed and inflexible mental attitude. It is difficult, if not impossible, to persuade the four to accept other ideas or to consider a different course from that which has been set. Such attempts should be avoided! You will see this person living a life of self-guidance and self-criticism, needing little interference from the outside world.

The Card

The four of clubs is a card of closely knit friendships and social capacities. It suggests that the client is loved and highly respected by those around him without his being aware of it. This implies that assistance may be obtained from unexpected quarters should it be needed.

Although this card symbolizes steady growth and often suggests a bond of affection which increases day by day, the client may feel lonely and abandoned because of a failure to notice appreciation from others. Modesty, restraint or vagueness can prevent this individual from openly expressing affection in a friendship which lies within reach. If that is the case, you could point out that more friendliness and interest in his environment could open doors to meaningful social employment. It should be stressed here that the client underestimates himself and is really capable of sincere friendship as well as being worthy of other's approaches. It would definitely enrich the client's life if he were more aware of the appreciation of others, but he in his turn must also endeavor to discover what is admirable and of value in his fellow men. Good health—one of his greatest problems—is of great importance to the four of clubs since he needs and uses a great deal of energy in all endeavors.

♣ ♣ ♣

CLUBS: intuition, sensitivity, spontaneity
FIVE: discord, restlessness, change
FIVE OF CLUBS: possibilities of change

FIVE OF CLUBS

Positive: fond of freedom, adventurous, curious, sensual

Negative: disagreeable, quarrelsome, loves competition, cruel, violent, possessed, extravagant and wasteful

Personal Characteristics

The energetic, money-wasting, emotional imbalance of the five of clubs is the cause of many disappointments, disagreements, and quarrels with friends and acquaintances. One inner voice may say, "Settle down, stay where you are, make something of it and be content." However, will the restless side of this person's nature be able to take this advice and act accordingly? Almost never! As a result of this instability, the five of clubs finds it exceedingly difficult to make long term compromises. In fact, immediate gratification is often pursued. Unfortunately, this on-the-spot satisfaction is not always attainable and the individual simply goes off to find it elsewhere. The five may not acknowledge that the discord is a part of the inner self and may blame the environment for any discontent.

The charming, almost magnetic side of the five of clubs can only be shown to full advantage if the world is faced in a friendly, open manner. Then windfalls and good fortune can be experienced, but the five must work for it—and often work is considered a limitation to personal freedom.

The Card

From earliest times, the five of clubs has been seen as a card which seeks harmony between old friends. However, there still exists the chance that a serious difference of opinion will cause the client much sorrow if no measure is taken to avoid it. This does not concern lovers' squabbles or marital disagreements. Rather, the difference of opinion is between the client and someone of the same sex, unless a picture card representing the opposite sex lies nearby. This card symbolizes rivalry, competition, emulation and jealousy. It warns the client not to make a show of personal success or envy others theirs.

Special Significance

If the five of clubs appears in the center of the spread, the client will encounter unsuspected enmity among colleagues. If unable to control anger caused by undeserved enmity, or giving no sign of exceptional understanding of this unfair situation, people previously considered friends will become estranged. The importance of the remaining cards in the layout determines the gravity of the situation in the long run.

If the five of clubs lies in one of the top corners of the spread, it concerns a quarrel which can be avoided. The reader will have to determine from the other cards how to persuade the client to get out of a situation which only brings sorrow and self-reproach.

Should the five of clubs appear in one of the bottom corners of the spread, the quarrel is most likely to concern one particular subject. In that case, malevolence on the part of another will cause the client disappointment with respect to a social project of great importance.

In the bottom left-hand corner, the disappointment can be the result of circumstances for which no one is responsible. In that case, the client should not attempt to blame anyone. Apparent loss of prestige, however, will by a roundabout way still appear to be useful if so indicated by the cards lying around the five of clubs.

♣   ♣   ♣

CLUBS: intuition, sensitivity, spontaneity

SIX: mediation, adaptation, understanding of life

SIX OF CLUBS: victory, unexpected good luck, cheerfulness

SIX OF CLUBS

Positive: benevolent, trustworthy, steadfast, victorious after conflict, impersonal, subservient, responsive, musical, humorous, well-traveled

Negative: proud, self-centered, cynical, meddlesome, jealous, distrustful, apathetic

Personal Characteristics

The six of clubs tries to maintain an impersonal attitude to life by being self-sacrificing. It is a responsive card, which in itself adds nothing to its own life or to that of others. The person will act in a friendly, neutral manner, unconcernedly allowing life to happen.

Although the six of clubs is a just card, it can seem to be cold or unfeeling because of its impersonal attitude. However distant the manner may seem, this is a person who really lives in a friendly and affectionate atmosphere. The mother has a lot of influence, causing the six to feel most comfortable around rather domineering women whose linear sense of purpose gives a familiar direction to activities pursued by the six. Always surviving periods of personal sorrow, depression or dejection with the help of an intellectual disposition, the six applies a great deal of energy to career. Actually work helps the pain go away. The six of clubs is a card of resurrection and is often associated with Easter.

Although the six of clubs may enjoy a busy social life, this is not a card symbolic of someone involved with empty-headed pleasures. The pleasure promised by the card should be seen as part of the lesson of living life. The six will change attitudes during the growth process. In some gypsy card games, the six of clubs indicates a journey or change of residence. The journeys taken by the six could be mental ones, and physical changes in residence may coincide with a change in world view. The outer manifestation in this case is reflective of an inner transformation.

The Card

The six of clubs is traditionally seen as a card of good luck, which, along with bringing increasing respect in social circles, symbolizes other advantages—such as financial gain, some increased security, or even the possibility of a new love. In the tarot deck, the six of clubs is sometimes represented by a merchant who is doling out alms to a begger—the sign of prosperity as well as a good heart—but the card also contains a warning against too much pride, condescension or jealousy.

Special Significance

If the ten of spades, the two of spades, or the five of diamonds is lying near the six of clubs, the client should aim for more balance between what is serious in life and what is looked for as a diversion. A harmonious balance needs to be restored.

CLUBS: intuition, sensitivity, spontaneity
SEVEN: insight, a turning-point
SEVEN OF CLUBS: warning against approaching disaster

SEVEN OF CLUBS

Positive: courageous, intelligent, calm, analytical, meticulous, farsighted

Negative: distant, nervous, depressed, vague, unreal, shy, addictive

Personal Characteristics

The seven of clubs represents the calm, intelligent, trustworthy, loyal worker who tends to remain behind the scenes. This individual works best in private, and leads a rather mundane and lonely existence, very often working for enough money to provide for daily needs. If the seven of clubs doesn't plan career moves carefully, plans for advancement may miscarry. Should this occur, there is a considerable possibility that this individual will sink into a depression and may even seek salvation in alcohol or other narcotics.

The seven of clubs is not easy to change or convince, and is mainly led by intuition—which seldom fails. The seven generally sees things coming far in advance. Although the seven of clubs knows many people, this card is often misunderstood by others. The seven enjoys being alone for this reason, even if being alone means that periods of severe inner conflict take place. Perhaps this indicates a person who "talks to himself."

The Card

The seven of clubs is a warning against imaginary progress, against attempts or plans that are not solidly constructed. Plans fail to take place in the last minute because the client has lightheartedly assumed that everything is in order. Not so. The client needs to be warned that the seven is not an indication of impending disaster, but that it stands as a warning to check plans more carefully.

The seven of clubs also indicates high aspirations. It also indicates that the individual may start many projects without finishing them. Jumping from one project to another will dissipate energy, and the project may be lost because it is not properly taken care of. If success is what your client is looking for, then some hard work still remains to be done.

Special Significance

If the seven of clubs lies between hearts, duty may be neglected for the pursuit of pleasure. If the card lies between diamonds, the client may be threatened with some financial chicanery, or underhanded practices at work may undermine safety in some manner.

The seven of clubs in the top left corner of a spread signifies that the goal is within reach, but in order to complete the process the client needs to be vigilant, conscientious, and will still need to invest a lot of energy in the project. Any tendency to give in too quickly, or to wallow in too much or too little self-confidence should be avoided.

In the top right corner, the seven of clubs indicates that the client is in some danger of suffering losses as a result of indifference or neglect. Your client may be counting on a successful outcome or may be too busy with other matters to expend the thought necessary for success of the project under question.

When the seven of clubs lies in the middle of the spread, it indicates that the client is not using all the means at his command. This is a card of high aspirations, and the client may be dissipating energy. Find out if the client is questioning you about one project while also having other "irons in the fire." If this is the case, the card serves as a warning that the project will not go well if it is not cared for.

In the bottom corners of a spread, the seven of clubs alludes to a specific situation rather than a general attitude. Placed with a picture card, the seven warns against a lack of thought or some indifference on the part of colleagues or staff. Advise your client to maintain control over any business enterprise that is being handled by others, especially if career image or finances are involved. The seven aligned with a picture card also indicates that the client should not reveal plans to others at this time, because too much optimism could cause unnecessary failure or needless setbacks in regard to the planned project or activity. The seven is always a warning against danger and is not a prophecy of approaching disaster—but the client must take care of business at this time.

♣ ♣ ♣

CLUBS: intuition, sensitivity, spontaneity
EIGHT: power, will, orgainzation
EIGHT OF CLUBS: striving for balance

EIGHT OF CLUBS

Positive: speed, tense activity, frankness, a broad outlook, friendly, understanding, generous, approaching a goal

Negative: slow, unstable, unbalanced, depressed, selfish, self-indulgent, spoiled, childish, sudden setbacks

Personal Characteristics

The eight of clubs is very social, and is often surrounded by many people. If situations threaten to get emotionally out of hand in a group, intuitive mental attitudes enables this individual to act realistically, although there is a tendency to become too involved in psychological implications. The eight of clubs can overcome practically any problem by means of inner strength, but needs time to accomplish this, and therefore spends long periods in a rut which knows no equal, waiting for or seeking the solution to the dissatisfaction. Usually something suddenly happens to wake or enlighten the eight as to the cause of the lethargy. This is naturally followed by a feeling of emotional harmony.

Financial conditions tend to fluctuate, and although it may not be rosy, there is always enough money to feel secure. Even though the eight of clubs has no valid reason to worry, there is a tendency to do so. The greatest difficulties for the eight of clubs lie in the emotional realm. Both male and female need to love or be loved, and both are sometimes the subject of jealousy and envy. However, the eights will never be without friends or admirers because they possess a gift of sublimating amorous feelings and finding happiness in friendships or work. There is a tendency to take on more than can be managed, which causes tension in order to honor some self-imposed obligation. The attempt to attain a balance needs to be recognized here.

The Card

In the traditional sense, the eight of clubs is a card of harmony and tranquil pleasue. Here is a philosophical spirit searching and finding beauty in such simple things as flowers, sunsets, books and friends. This is the card of the gentle dreamer, although it only represents one (probably hidden) aspect of the client's personality. There is also a tendency to reject material comfort and luxury in favor of fulfilling the demands made on a mental and spiritual level.

Special Significance

The client who has the eight of clubs in a layout has been blessed—for this card is protective against all the numerous vicissitudes of life. Its energy renders negatives harmless. The eight of clubs promises happiness which will increase over the years.

The presence of this card in the center of a layout signifies above all that the client should rely upon inner spiritual strength. This is particularly applicable when diamonds dominate the layout, since the client then runs the risk of financial and business affairs absorbing so much energy that true enjoyment of the beauty of life will not be possible.

CLUBS: intuition, sensitivity, spontaneity
NINE: desire, the grand passion, philanthropy
NINE OF CLUBS: emotional tension

NINE OF CLUBS

Positive or negative: strength, power of endurance, success after revolt and battle, recovery following illness, victory after worry and fear, knowledge that change provides the greatest security and stability

Personal Characteristics

The content of this card can best be described as "learning to control the emotions," which is no easy task for the nine of clubs in view of his heavy load. This card has a strong impersonal tendency and because of this contrast, when the emotions are strongly self-oriented, the nine of clubs may become ill from the tension caused by severe inner conflict. The future then appears very black and the cares of the entire world seem to be pressing down. Since the nine of clubs has a tendency to see love relationships as the aim of life, there is a considerable chance that as soon as there is a romantic involvement, hardly any achievement (or none at all) occurs on the job. Emotional conflicts may even bring about psychosomatic illnesses that could cause lengthy periods of disability or the nervous system could be affected.

The Card

The nine of clubs is a hypernervous, romantic, unconventional card with a warm concern for people and their mutual relationships. This is why the nine of clubs is drawn to the group life. The size of the group is not important as long as our nine is able to care for the sick, the maladjusted or the handicapped. This individual is someone capable of being both a hanger-on and a participant—and both traits can manifest at the same time! This card also signifies one who is dogmatic or superstitious.

The nine of clubs is not particularly attracted to marriage because personal ties are too oppressive. An impersonal contact with different people seems better, for this card may not want to be bound to one specific person.

On the path through life the nine usually comes into contact with one or more older, wiser, friendly mother and/or father figures who can give structure, security and restore any waning sense of self-confidence. Only then can the nine work with the pleasure and success essential for personal security.

Special Significance

If the nine of diamonds appears in a layout with the nine of clubs, financial advantage can be expected. If the client's work lies in the field of fine arts, it signifies an important or a good contract. In business, a promotion or improvement of position lies ahead. If the nine of hearts is in the same spread, the nine of clubs can bring recognition, fame and applause. There is the possibility of happiness as a reward for strenuous work. However, if the nine of spades appears with the nine of clubs, eventual success will be preceded by setbacks, struggle, and perhaps even fatal threats. When reading this spread, keep the question in perspective.

If the nine of clubs appears in the top left-hand corner of a layout, success depends on the speedy intervention of the client. What is sought lies within grasp, but the client must immediately set to work in the right manner, otherwise it may be lost. The nine of clubs in the bottom corner limits the promised success to one specific situation. If the client takes advantage of this knowledge, it can bring financial reward, fame or recognition. The cards in the same row as the nine of clubs will provide a decisive answer concerning the nature of the enterprise, the people involved, the obstacles to be overcome and the circumstances which will be of help to the client.

CLUBS: intuition, sensitivity,
  spontaneity
TEN: success, completion
TEN OF CLUBS: complete
  development through
  new insight

TEN OF CLUBS

Positive: self-control, curiosity, astonishment, idealism, ambition, loyalty, and intelligence

Negative: uncertainty, mutiny, maliciousness, deceit, cruelty, destruction, selfishness, oppression, slander

Personal Characteristics

This card represents the manner in which private circumstances and business activities influence each other. The appearance of a ten of clubs in a spread frequently indicates that a business is being run from home and is filled with irregularities and inconveniences. The domestic life suffers on account of the business and vice versa.

There is a good chance of success in business affairs here because the ten of clubs has an active intelligence, accurate judgement and a high energy level. For this reason, this individual feels most at ease with the tension involved in a quick turnover, often participating in mail order companies, telephone ordering, and shopping services.

In a personal sense, this card is most active at about thirty-six years of age. Spiritual maturity will only develop in middle age. In the meantime there are periods of restlessness and irresponsible behavior. The need for love and security causes the ten of clubs to make unnecessary sacrifices. This in turn precipitates personality crises which have a scattering effect and undermine the direction of this card. The changeable image indicated by this card has something immature about it, and the ten of clubs, therefore, may also evoke the image of a boy full of wonderment and inexperience. This person has an astonishing number of ideals, along with a desire to investigate everything, but also present is a feeling of insecurity and the tendency to shrink away from reality. As long as character and personality are yet unformed, this card will remain a barrel of contradictions. When reading for this person, the reader needs to keep in mind the age of the individual.

The Card

This figure does not represent the client, but someone through whom the client can gauge the alternating joys and sorrows of youth. If the client is of advanced age, the card will possibly refer to a protégé, a son or daughter, or even a grandchild. If the client is young, the card frequently indicates a friend who is closely linked to the client. The client may enter a whole new world of experience through the person represented by the ten of clubs—acquiring new interests and awakening slumbering ambitions and ideals. Life will be enriched but everything will not be easy. Misunderstandings and clashes may arise on a personal level. The relationship may seem one-sided, and should this be the case, it signifies that the client has failed in some way.

The ten of clubs may be understanding, loyal, idealistic and intelligent, but an inquisitive mind can often land him into an adventure which turns out quite differently than the one anticipated. Disappointment may cause rebellions, and the ten's action taken may cause the client sorrow or may arouse disapproval. The older client should remember that it is not necessary to mold the ten into another image, nor can the client protect another from certain life experiences. The older client can give advice, opening new doors for intellectual development or for establishing values, but must also avoid becoming emotionally dependent on the ten.

The ten of clubs may also indicate something that once interested the client will come to life again. Perhaps pleasure will be found in searching for old childhood friends, or perhaps a long-forgotten ambition will resurface. These activities will usually be expressed in some form of creativity in the arts, writing, painting, music or drama.

The ten could be symbolized by a human figure reaching back to the past with one arm while stretching the other out toward the future. This indicates a new life being built on the old foundation, forming a continuity between youth, adulthood, and old age. The gypsies called this the card of adoption. This can be taken literally in some cases, but it generally concerns the adoption of new ideas or new inspiration which brings fresh interest to life.

♣　♣　♣

CLUBS: intuition, sensitivity,
　　spontaneity
JACK: idealism, youth
JACK OF CLUBS: the hard-
　　working, idealistic young
　　friend (male or female)

JACK OF CLUBS

Positive: proud, strong, just, prepared to help, friendly, good-humored, quick

Negative: immovable, intolerant, moody, quick-tempered, cowardly, calculating, cruel

Personal Characteristics

The jack of clubs usually indicates a hard-working young person. The card selfom refers to the client, but rather someone who is favorably disposed toward your client. To determine the sex of the jack of clubs, we should look at the eyes on the card itself. If the eyes face the center of the spread, the jack symbolizes the sex opposite to that of the client. If the jack looks away from the center, the card represents someone of the same sex.

The client will probably not hold the jack of clubs in high esteem because this card is seen as too simple, too dull, or too serious. In the eyes of a female, the jack is insufficiently lively as a boyfriend, and as a girlfriend, this card represents someone who is too silly. From the male point of view, the jack of clubs could represent a girl he knows but who has never been seen in any romantic light. Or it could signify a friend whose loyality is taken as a matter of course.

The jack of clubs is, in fact, a rock in the surf who will only show strength in times of need. Beneath a somewhat ordinary exterior lies a loyal, generous, self-sacrificing individual with many hidden talents. Content to play second fiddle, the jack often intentionally withholds superior knowledge and accomplishment so as to put the client in the best possible light.

With a slow tempo, the jack of clubs can curb the client's overimpulsiveness and actually be a guide to better achievement. Taken as a whole, the advice of the jack of clubs is sensible and practical, but the protective precautions will sometimes have an irritating effect on your client because of the jack's lack of tact. Honesty impels the jack to say bluntly what he has on his mind.

The Card

The presence of the jack of clubs in a layout indicates that the client has someone near whom he does not sufficiently value, someone helping his interests, who offers inspiration and support without any need for reward. The characterization of the jack of clubs as young should not be taken too literally. The term harmless is probably more suitable. If the jack of clubs and the client are the same age, the jack of clubs may appear older than he is due to his voluntary acceptance of second place.

The appearance of the jack of clubs draws the client's attention to a one-sided situation of affection and attachment. Perceiving, esteeming and accepting the characteristics of a friend can make the client realize that many roads lead to Rome, and that tolerance is an indispensable part of true warmth and affection. The jack of clubs may also indicate a threatening crisis in which this friendship will play a decisive role.

CLUBS: intuition, sensitivity,
  spontaneity
QUEEN: reacting, judging
QUEEN OF CLUBS: practical,
  intutive

QUEEN OF CLUBS

Positive: great ability to adjust, tenacity, calmness, great magnetism, warm, composed, violent in regard to love or anger

Negative: cannot bear contradiction, quick to take offense, stupid, cruel, vengeful, domineering, theatrical, perfidious, superficial, false

Personal Characteristics

The queen of clubs has all the desirable qualities for an interesting social life. She playfully steals men's hearts, but none of them can either captivate or understand her. She has a warm, friendly, engaging manner. She cannot be surpassed as a fellow traveler or partner, for she conceals a calculating mind and a worldly awareness under a lighthearted exterior. She appears to be a flirt, but don't be fooled. She is really very sensitive, taking offense quickly. She is moody and it may be hard for others to understand that she can be sympathetic one minute and so angry the next that she is capable of causing violent or embarrasing scenes.

This person is unpredictable, inspired by the whim of the moment. She loves to go to parties, likes to dance and travel. She is particular about her dress and loves to shop for clothes and luxuries. She adores everything that is beautiful, and needs to be admired for her own beauty. Although she is capable of making many friendships, they don't last long for she also has a need to test her friends. This is caused by a basic insecurity, and the queen is really testing where she stands.

Men who fall in love with her will not know where they stand, as her personality is multi-faceted. One day she is straight-forward, the next day she is coy. Her depressions, tears, or violent outbursts of anger may frighten people. She does need someone to understand and love her for who she is— someone who can accept all her moods and variations in behavior. She has plenty to give in terms of devotion when her heart is won, and her calculating, yet intuitive mind can be a great help in a partnership.

The Card

The queen of clubs indicates the presence of a warm and friendly woman who is more worldly than your client might suspect. She is fickle—being friendly one minute and capable of testing your friendship the next. She may cut your relationship completely if she feels insecure.

If this card represents the person for whom you are doing the reading, she may need counselling about how she projects herself to others, or about developing an inner sense of security that will alleviate the emotional outbursts, or the testing of friends and loved ones. If she represents a person in the life of a man you are reading for, her character will be described for him. He may need to hear about her moodiness, and about the inner capabality of devotion, so he can make up his mind about her. If she is important in some business alliance with your client, you should share information about how to handle this woman so that any projects that have been started will be completed.

Special Significance

In her relationships with other women, the queen of clubs prefers her own type. Such friendships are normally of short duration and full of bickering. The queen of clubs is easy-going, cheerful, and always looking for something exciting to do. She is therefore capable of getting along well with the queen of hearts, for this queen approves and supports the queen of clubs. The queen of spades instinctively dislikes the queen of clubs. The presence of both cards in a reading indicate that a conflict will take place between two women described by these cards, and that the queen of spades will probably win as she has greater insight and better self-control.

If a female has the queen of clubs lying in the center of a layout, it is usually a reflection of herself or the difficulties in which she finds herself. If another queen or jack is there as well, the life of the queen of clubs will be modified accordingly. If a male client has a queen of clubs lying in the center of his spread, the woman who plays a major role in his life will have the characteristics symbolized by this card. If the queen of clubs is in the top right corner of a spread of either man or woman, this type of woman will be somehow drawn into his or her affairs. If the queen of clubs lies in the top left corner, the client will soon be forced to take a clear stand in regard to such a woman. The remaining cards in the layout can provide a decisive answer as to the role she will play in the client's life.

The appearance of the queen of clubs in a bottom corner warns of a situation of deceit. The client should be advised to anaylize the facts carefully, for it would not be a good idea to rely on vague impressions or take someone else's word about this woman. If the nine of hearts lies next to the queen of clubs, it can indicate that this queen will bring the client plenty of excitement.

♣ ♣ ♣

CLUBS: intuition, sensitivity, spontaneity
KING: vitality, authority
KING OF CLUBS: the realization of ideals

KING OF CLUBS

Positive: friendly, generous, proud, quick and impetuous

Negative: cruel, malicious, short-tempered, violent, indolent and stupid

Personal Characteristics

Although this is a card of great power, self-assertion and determination, the king of clubs is not personally aware of his power. He is a man of many interests, one who is cheerful on the outside, but closed and reserved on the inside. He is not easy to assess, and a natural reserve can conceal his real feelings so well that he may appear to be secretive. He has a very strict code of idealistic humanitarian values, which may not be understood. He does not deviate from his standards one inch. Because he is sensitive to the outside world, he may appear cynical, autocratic, or even hard or cruel. Deep in his heart, this is the knight who rebels against injustice, someone who is always ready to help the oppressed. The protective shell around his personality is probably there because feelings have been hurt in the past, and this wall helps him cover hurt feelings.

The Card

This card indicates a person who possesses a great deal of natural talent. He symbolizes someone who works for a living in order to earn enough money to do what he wants to do. It is important to note that this is not a loyal worker who works his fingers to the bone—this is more the card of a man who works so he can enjoy his hobbies later.

The king of clubs often lives alone. He may not have a permanent relationship, but he would like to know a warm and understanding woman. He has difficulty letting people know he likes them, so in matters of love he is easily intimidated and plays a passive role reminiscent of the country song "But You Don't Know Me." This man places women on a pedestal, which also doesn't help develop relationships! He is extremely sensitive and would be appreciative of any warmth shown him.

Special Significance

There is a natural affinity between the queen of diamonds and the king of clubs. Her realism can bring his best points to the fore and she can help him utilize his many talents in some constructive way. Her drive will push him to greater activity as well as challanging him to grow.

The queen of spades is by nature hostile to the king of clubs. Her cool and distant behavior or her hidden passions may prevent him from using his gifts. He may be spellbound by her, and a relationship between the two of them may cause them both to withdraw into themselves.

If your client is male, and the king of clubs appears in the center of the spread, it will indicate your client's personality. If the king of clubs lies in a corner of the spread, the characteristics are more apt to be those of an intimate friend—a collegue or companion—but not a member of the family.

If the king of clubs appears in the center for a female client, you will know that this type of man will play an important role in her life. If he appears in one of the corners, the king indicates someone who does not play a terribly important role.

If both the king of clubs and the queen of spades appear in the same layout, this may be an indicator of domestic trouble, or it may even indicate an impending divorce or separation between two people. You will learn more about the situation by examining the cards that represent conflict or unhappiness to see if they lie between the king and the queen.

HEARTS

HEARTS: love, self-sacrifice, service
ACE: endeavoring, ruling, wanting, individuality
ACE OF HEARTS: desire for affection, feeling

ACE OF HEARTS

Positive: cheerfulness, pleasure, happiness, fertility, receptivity, summer

Negative: poverty, suspicious, scheming, cunning, overindulgent

Personal Characteristics

On the material level, the ace of hearts is almost always in trouble. He may have to toil for his entire life, or learn to live on a shoestring. However, since the ace is not really a materialist, he remains undaunted by life's meager circumstances and needs little to be happy.

The ace of hearts may seem moody to others, for those he finds sweet, honest and beautiful one minute may appear to be cruel, disloyal or ugly soon after. Although capable of clarity of purpose and personal integrity, the ace can undermine his own values and goals by allowing too many people to influence his lifestyle. If this is done, the fear of competition may arise—causing a cunning, calculating and suspicious person to develop. Ironically, this attitude often evokes the exact response from others that he is trying to avoid. He may suffer emotional disappointments, blaming those disappointments on others, seeing people as untrustworthy, cold or manipulative.

This ace needs to search his own heart while learning to trust in his inner responses, rather than trying to overidealize other people. The ace is strong enough to overcome obstacles if he becomes self-disciplined, and doesn't waste too much of his inherent strength on sensual pleasures. Without this self-awareness, the aces performance will not achieve the success possible.

The Card

The ace of hearts is a card which promises pleasure, cheerfulness, love and fertility. If placed unfavorably in the layout, it can, however, be a warning against waste, loss, or sacrifice of spiritual values in favor of more fleeting pleasures. Like all aces, it also possesses explosive power. A strong romantic bond, birth or rebirth of faith, or spiritual happiness may be heralded by it. According to tradition, the ace of hearts is the card of young love—a promise of matrimony and children. However, the card should be read in context, as love has many faces and can be interpreted in broader terms.

Special Significance

If the ace of hearts is flanked by clubs, the joy will be less spectacular and more peaceful or harmonious. If diamonds dominate the layout, the joy will take the form of luck in business or the client will gain a great deal of pleasure from work. Whenever the ace of hearts appears, it should always be interpreted as an encouragement to happiness with others. It also warns that the client is not using natural talents to the fullest capacity.

Where the ace of hearts dominates the spread, the client should be advised to increase the social circle—to allow new people into life on a friendly basis. This person can excel in social work, pastoral care, or by working in the field of education, as these occupations bring one into touch with many people. The card indicates an ability to help others bring their natural talents to the surface.

If a two of spades lies between the ace of hearts and a picture card, it can signify a barrier to fruitful contact with others, but this barrier can be removed. The reader could advise the client of this problem, because the client could then find a solution and live more comfortably.

If a nine of spades lies next to the ace of hearts, or if one of the corners is blocked by a nine of spades, the client should be warned against a situation that may threaten personal happiness. Or the card may indicate that your client is so filled with self-content that others are annoyed or hurt by some blithe stepping on toes. Your client's optimism may even cause a reckless attitude in regard to personal possessions. If this is the case, the current situation should be viewed more seriously, so as to insure future happiness.

If the ace of hearts lies in the center of the layout, joy will be an aspect of the client's personality. If a number of picture cards or tens are present in the spread, your client will have a chance to make new or pleasant social contacts. The client may be the center of attention, or be the beneficiary of more respect from peers than is presently considered. When the ace of hearts lies in the bottom left of a spread, it means that the client is the object of someone's love, admiration or glorification, but is completely unaware of it. If the cards in the middle of the spread are spades, the client may feel unloved, either because of personal shyness, cynicism, or a fear of being unlovable—which will make close relationships with other people rather difficult.

HEARTS: love, self-sacrifice, service

TWO: being together, going together, working together

TWO OF HEARTS: joy from working together

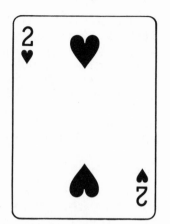

TWO OF HEARTS

Positive: love and harmony between man and woman in the broadest sense of the word; equilibrium, peace, tranquil joy, pleasure, warm friendships

Negative: foolishness, dissolution, decay, depression, disappointment

Personal Characteristics

Most heart cards respond to the world instinctively and emotionally. This is particularly true of the two of hearts. Awareness of emotions doesn't extend very far. Unless this person brings about a change by thinking more deeply about personal motivation, unconscious responses to emotions will really run the personality.

The two of hearts is no hero. This individual can not be called either great nor impressive, but is nevertheless well liked by a wide variety of friends. Fond of company, this individual is friendly, easy, entertaining, a social drinker, but underneath the sociability is a melancholy undertone. Perhaps this card places too much importance on feelings. Sometimes feelings are expressed in an overly exaggerated or melodramatic manner, often manipulating others into doing what the two wants done. So we could say that the two is very sensitive, but needs to learn how to use this sensitivity in a productive way. Once this is learned, problems can be easily solved, as the two of hearts has a stable inner core, and can function as a valued member of society.

The two of hearts can be a good buyer, mediator, interpreter, or foreign agent of some kind. Although (like all the twos), this card has a strongly domestic nature, career involvement may take the two far from home. Circumstances often conspire to force the two to stand firm on both feet, and the two is so uncomfortable about this, that it makes us see this card as a brittle or tough person. If the two perseveres, the apparent toughness or brittleness can be worked through, and a person capable of working with others will emerge.

The Card

According to tradition, the two of hearts indicates a love letter or a piece of good news. In fact, this card really has a much deeper significance, for it suggests that happiness or joy can be found in one's back yard so to speak. We all tend to ignore the daily pleasures that are right there to appreciate, and this card suggests that the client should look for more of that.

The appearance of the two of hearts may indicate that your client is missing opportunities, valuable contacts, or social successes because attention is so future oriented that the present is going by unseen.

Special Significance

When the two of hearts lies next to a picture card signifying a member of the opposite sex, it indicates that someone close is prepared to provide love and care if given the opportunity to do so. If a picture card symbolizing a same sex person is next to the two of hearts, your client may be overlooking a friendship which could mean a great deal.

When the two of hearts is flanked by diamonds, the client needs to look for opportunities for profit or promotion. A layout dominated by clubs indicates that connections or conviviality is available if your client will make some attempt to notice what is going on. When the two of hearts lies between other hearts, it may indicate an individual who is overly involved in pursuing the pleasure of the moment and foretells someone who doesn't go after anything of lasting value.

However the client is using this energy, the two of hearts brings an opportunity to enrich life. Laudable and long-term ideals do not need to be thrown overboard. Opportunites lie within reach and can provide the stuff which dreams are made of.

HEARTS: love, self-sacrifice, service

THREE: uncertainty, personal development

THREE OF HEARTS: uncertainty concerning physical welfare

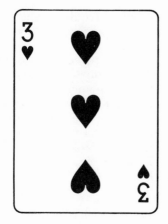

THREE OF HEARTS

Positive: fertility, hospitality, pleasure, sensuality, passivity, friendship, gentleness, mercy

Negative: doubt, triviality, laziness, addiction, disappointment, deception, panic. The good things in life should be reviewed with reserve and enjoyed in moderation.

Personal Characteristics

The three of hearts is born to work, but a gentle, passive character and an inclination to a life of ease usually lands a routine job or a monotonous existence. This doesn't appear to matter to the three since pleasure is often sought in the proverbial "wine, women and song" syndrome. In view of the fact that the "good things" in life are enjoyed too much, the next phase of concern is the result of dissipation, so the three of hearts may be coping with some kind of health problem. And the three can be really imaginative when it comes to illnesses, being able to think up, as it were, a new ailment for every day of the month! Although the lack of health isn't really serious, it should not be dismissed altogether either, as there may be something to the complaints.

As far as doctors are concerned, the three doubts them regularly, and goes from one doctor to the next, looking for cures. This person may also experiment with all kinds of medicines which may not have been prescribed. This card also indicates an interest in natural cures, seeking unusual remedies that basically relate to Mother Nature. However, it is wise to keep in mind that discontent may be the cause of some of the physical troubles, and that the cause of illness may relate to dissatisfaction, or inner turmoil may be related to unexpressed energy.

The three needs a good education in order to be free. When this person is well established in regard to a career, freedom can be maintained more easily as the ability to spontaneously respond to life is more able to operate. If education is lacking, the three tends to be much more cautious and careful in regard to the future, as well as in general activities. A lack of education may also cause this person to look for personal security in some mindless job, which will also have an effect on health and well-being.

The Card

The three of hearts signifies a disappointment in love, a setback in work, or a mistake in judgement. The appearance of this card is a warning that the way is not smooth for your client—there are unanticipated pitfalls ahead. The card is also an indication of self-deceit. Your client may secretly feel that he is his own worst enemy, or that a fear of change is the cause of the trouble he finds himself in. The client may be trying to find reasons to avoid reality on some level, or may be merely hoping that the problem will just go away. Anything that is oppressing should be looked at, for if inertia, hesitation and indecisiveness continue, the difficulties will become an intolerable burden.

The three of hearts symbolizes a promise of better times, but happiness, success and prosperity depend on the courage and determination that the client can mobilize. A disappointment in love can provide the opportunity to talk things out in a bad relationship. A temporary set-back at work can lead to some honest self-reflection.

Special Significance

When the three of hearts is preceeded by the nine of hearts, it signifies that an immediate decision must be made or some action must be taken in order to insure future comfort. In such a case, you could recommend that your client take some kind of action in regard to the problem needing to be solved. Some conscious choice is required now. The danger lies not so much in making a mistake as in walking unthinkingly into a situation from which it will be difficult to extricate oneself later on.

♥ ♥ ♥

HEARTS: love, self-sacrifice, service
FOUR: structure and building
FOUR OF HEARTS: satisfaction and pleasure in work or relationships

FOUR OF HEARTS

Positive: pleasure, honesty, justice, balance, sociability, discriminating mind, a willingness to help others

Negative: self-centeredness, indolence, lack of perseverance

Personal Characteristics

The four of hearts is a person who is extremely idealistic, someone who has an all embracing and ever-present sense of the emotional ideal. This card symbolizes a person who walks with his head in the clouds. On the other hand, the four has a good sense of integrity, justice and tolerance. Accurate judgment and a strong intuitive sense help this individual balance idealism. With these natural characteristics it is not unusual to find this person in the position of judge, advisor, leader or director. The social services also provide interesting work that corresponds to the idealistic bent.

When the idealism is not well grounded, the card can be self-centered. Sometimes credit can be taken for hard work done by others—for teamwork may be considered as personal accomplishment. Or a job may be left unfinished because personal interest has waned.

No matter what the career is, this person needs to be involved in some charitible work. The four may be caught up in the theatre or film, or may pursue an artistic career. If this is so, time should also be devoted to groups that need help. This is also a card that indicates the natural gift of healing. When the four of hearts uses this gift, amazing cures can be affected.

In personal relationships, the four needs a strong and harmonious involvement in order to be completely happy. However, others may not understand this card, as love may be felt from a more universally oriented standpoint, while family or intimates may feel left out.

The Card

The four of hearts suggests that there is a chance to feel happy doing one's work. The work indicated by the card may be the client's present vocation or something that the client wishes to do. The four of hearts can be a card of self-denial, indicating that some choices must be made, or there must be some willingness to sacrifice for something. The reward for such a sacrifice is not likely to lie in the financial sphere, although there is a considerable chance that life will be financially enriched by services rendered to others.

The four of hearts may represent children or very young people. The implication here is that working in youth clubs or with school organizations may give the client some intense fulfillment. On the other hand, working with people who are in the youth of old age may also provide this fulfillment.

Special Significance

The four of hearts flanked by diamonds indicates that voluntary work could lead to an improvement in position, raise in salary, or unexpected gifts. When the layout is filled with clubs, the way lies open to new and rewarding social contacts. If other hearts or picture cards from any suit are closely connected to the four of hearts by position, there is a chance of making a new friend or of starting a new romance.

HEARTS: love, self-sacrifice, service
FIVE: discord, restlessness, change
FIVE OF HEARTS: setbacks, disappointments in matters of love

FIVE OF HEARTS

Positive: willing to sacrifice, trustworthy, helpful, loyal, hard-working

Negative: disappointments, unfriendly, unexpected interference and difficulty, setbacks in matters of love, the end of love affairs or friendships, malice, treachery, sorrow, repentance which come too late

Personal Characteristics

The restlessness inherent in all fives is not caused by a need for freedom nor dissatisfaction with environment in the case of the five of hearts. It is principally a result of a compulsion to improve the life of loved ones.

The cross borne by this card is formed by bonds of affection. Seldom fickle, foolish or disloyal, and generally steadfast and full of love, this card is involved with the anxiety and heartache caused by loved ones. No sacrifice is too great, no task too difficult, no privation too overwhelming when it comes to loved ones. The five of hearts will frequently be confronted with the broken affairs, divorces, suffering, illness, or poverty of those near and dear. Although the five of hearts may try to offer relief, this help rarely results in any change.

The five of hearts is often involved in travel, either for pleasure or for business. This card enjoys work and needs to keep busy. Holding a routine job or leading a humdrum existence may cause this individual to wind up a peevish grumbler, a drudge or a fatalist.

If the five is female, she will sacrifice herself uncritically for her husband. If the five refers to a male, he may be overly influenced by his mother. In both cases, marriage may be clouded by the disapproval of others, with divorce the end result.

The Card

The five of hearts is a card of disappointment, tears, or futile remorses. It can signify the end of a love affair, or the relinquishing of a long-cherished plan or attitude. In the end, however, the sorrow is usually not too deep or long-lasting, because the client really knows that the situation was a foolish one. Vanity may be wounded, but wounds caused by vanity do not leave lasting scars. The card may also signify that the grief felt by the client is also bringing a sense of relief.

When a disappointing romance is ended, a one-sided friendship is terminated, or illusive ideas are grounded by harsh reality, the way is now open for a more positive future. If unfortunate incidents are kept in perspective, your client may be able to turn this into a good experience—called a lesson well learned.

♥   ♥   ♥

HEARTS: love, self-sacrifice, service
SIX: mediation, adaptation, understanding of life
SIX OF HEARTS: imperturbable kindness

SIX OF HEARTS

Positive: complacency, contentment, ease, calm, satisfaction of sexual desires, fulfillment, the start of a steady increase, journeys over water

Negative: vanity, egoism, arrogance, prejudice, interference, ingratitude

Personal Characteristics

The six of hearts represents a peaceful, friendly person—well-balanced, trustworthy and devoted—one who will seldom be overcome by violent storms of emotion. This card dislikes being hurried, and takes time to study, listen to, and evaluate the people and things in the environment before drawing any conclusions. By trying to understand, put in order, or clear away any irregularities or problems that may come to light, and even though this quality is seldom appreciated, the six of hearts is a trusted worker.

In vainer moments, this card would like to be seen as the benefactor of mankind. Somewhat languid and indolent, this individual often prefers to sit comfortably by the fireside rather than seeking pleasure outside the home. A certain amount of complacency is not foreign, and a tendency to interfere in other people's business without invitation, albeit with the best of intentions, needs to be curbed.

This card usually signifies a person with a one-track mind, and it is near impossible to arouse interest in anything off that track! Whatever holds the interest is analyzed and understood in depth. As a result of this singlemindedness, the six is often an expert, although recognition of this expertise is not always financial. This doesn't really matter to a six. This individual knows exactly what he or she wants or likes and does exactly that—in an inperturbable manner. At worst, this card may be found in institutions or homes for criminals or the disturbed.

The six of hearts doesn't look for revenge. In such situations, the six tenders understanding and forgiveness, while trying to overcome difficulties using affection and concern. It can hardly be surprising to hear that this is sometimes called the "Christmas card."

A levelheaded, pleasant nature, along with a fondness for luxury and easy living, sometimes creates the impression that this person doesn't reciprocate love. Nothing could be less true. If, for example, the six of hearts must leave home for some time, a temporary "home" is created—all kinds of small trifles and familiar gewgaws are brought along to remind this individual of home. Family photos are packed in the wallet and family bonds are carried in the heart. Home and family are of the utmost importance to the six. Not caring for change in career or in domestic life, this is a convivial, easy, tolerant person—with some small, forgivable sins—who takes life as it comes and is content.

The six of hearts can be associated with well-to-do people who have inherited or who will inherit from the father's side of the family.

Special Significance

If the six of hearts lies in the middle of a spread, the client will have to make a choice in the near future. If the card lies in the top left-hand corner, the choice is open. In this case, the reader should look at the cards in the right-hand corner to see if a better path is available to the client. If the six of hearts appears in a bottom corner, it is possible that the ladder leads to a favorable situation, even though that situation may be temporary.

The Card

The six of hearts can best be seen as a ladder on which the client climbs the path to happiness. Several routes lead to success, fulfillment of a long-cherished dream, or a longlasting love—but all require hard work and sacrifice.

The client may feel that the end result is not worth the effort if the six shows up in the reading. Or—no matter how hard one tries, success is incomplete. This client should be cautioned to guard against impatience, irritability and pessimism. The six of hearts can be read as a signal that the client is a step nearer a major goal and risks total failure if shortcuts are attempted at this stage.

♥ ♥ ♥

HEARTS: love, self-sacrifice, service
SEVEN: insight, a turning point
SEVEN OF HEARTS: difference of opinion between sweethearts

SEVEN OF HEARTS

Positive: affection, devotion, magnetism

Negative: vanity, deception, illusory success, addiction, drunkenness, guilt, mendacity, unfulfilled promises, licentiousness, prostitution, deterioration of love and friendship

Personal Characteristics

The seven of hearts is a card of contradictions. On the one hand, it signifies a person who is deeply convinced that all difficulties in life can be solved with devotion, affection and love. This sense of security, combined with a not inconsiderable personal charm, attracts the most divergent, insecure, fickle, suspicious, jealous people upon whom the seven willingly wastes time and affection. Such an expenditure of energy often leads to dramatic emotional crises which may reveal the jealousy and suspicion present underneath the seven of heart's generosity.

On the other hand, the essential attitude of the seven of hearts is one of service. This card is by nature prepared to take on responsibility for the spiritual welfare of others and is often connected with boarding, monastic or convent schools or some other kind of secular education. This person has great need of some kind of spiritual norm against which to test the validity of quixotic adventures.

The seven of hearts must learn to use personal powers according to some code of ethics because there is a tendency to force things, to smash hindrances without respect for other people involved, to bend—and if necessary—to break the will-power of others if personal interests are in question.

The best which the seven of hearts can offer finds expression in a large group with humanistic ideals. This is a facile, charismatic speaker, and an inspried propagandist, who is able to sway an audience and move them to action. Unfortunately, the seven may waste a large part of this natural power—and even life—drifting from one job to another, moving from place to place and bearing little responsibility, while searching vaguely for some immediate satisfaction.

The sensitive, highly emotional seven of hearts is really a martyr's card. If personal interests are not sacrificed to a good cause or group endeavor, disappointment, jealousy and sorrow in love, or suspicion of some kind will plague the individual. As long as the seven is in a position serving others, recognition and respect can be attained. This is the seven at its best and happiest.

The Card

The seven of hearts is the traditional card signifying a lovers' quarrel. (It is also a card of belief and trust, symbolized by the clasped hands of children.) The quarrel it may signify may be a squall which actually clears the air, resulting in a clearer understanding between lovers. Whenever the seven of hearts appears, however, the client should be warned to keep an eye on the tongue—so to speak—or an unbridgable gap may be created in a relationship.

The term lovers' quarrel should not be taken too literally. It can just as easily refer to a difference of opinion between other closely connected people—such as a husband and wife, mother and daughter, or intimate friends. Where passions have the upper hand, the discord can take on serious proportions. The presence of the nine or ten of spades, or the ten of clubs urges the client to think before speaking.

Special Significance

If the seven of hearts lies in the middle of the spread, it indicates that the client is too gullible, or tends to let things get out of hand. Thoughtlessness or a fear of conflict can cause a loss of a good friendship, or domestic happiness could be gambled away. The card signifies a time to renew feelings for those people cherished by the client, as friendship, love and loyalty need to be reciprocal.

The appearance of the seven of hearts in a left-hand corner indicates that someone else needs to be supported and cherished by the client. If the card lies on the bottom left corner, this person is probably too timid, too awkward, or too overawed by the client to make emotional needs known. Feelings may be hidden behind sharp words or nitpicking, and the client should be advised that in such a situation, the best way to handle it would be by using kindness and a lot of tact! Whatever the situation is, it needs to be discussed—and a serious argument can be avoided by a discussion.

If the seven of hearts is found on the right side of the spread, the situation is reversed. It is the client who is dependent on someone, and the client is trying to conceal these feelings. In such a case, the client could be counselled to strengthen the existing relationship in a constructive way, rather than using sarcasm to cover fear. Objectivity usually brings what one wants much faster than false dealings and evasion.

HEARTS: love, self-sacrifice, service

EIGHT: power, will, organization

EIGHT OF HEARTS: behind-the-scenes leadership

EIGHT OF HEARTS

Positive: devotion to duty, industry, friendship, calmness, tenderness, tolerance

Negative: depression, indifference, nonchalance, lack of balance, moodiness, suspicion, boredom, lethargy, indolence, sloth

Personal Characteristics

The key phrase for the eight of hearts could be "Rising above all difficulties by means of intelligent insight." Devotion to duty is inscribed on this person's daily menu in gold letters! The eight works steadily without always realizing why. Although a hard worker, the card is not always consistent. Regularly putting health in jeopardy by suddenly working like a maniac in order to meet a deadline, in some cases the eight is merely motivated by a desire for respect and money—which is really a form of vanity. The eight cannot stand to be overlooked.

As soon as some money can be put aside (sometimes even before that) the eight buys land or houses because security is equated to owning property. The card indicates a considerable chance of inheritance from parents or of help from members of the family, although the mother is often a source of irritation and worry.

The eight of hearts is a friendly, calm but somewhat moody person who goes through life in a relatively relaxed manner. The card is naive and does not expect trouble. Therefore, the eight appears to be easygoing, maybe even slovenly and somewhat inattentive. The person gives an impression of being easily manipulated and duped. However, a sixth sense for this kind of underestimation of character is present in the eight, which also causes an indignant response. Those who think the eight is so naive will learn that this person is not a fool!

The Card

The eight of hearts represents a gift. This may be a gift that is either received or given by the client. The position of the card in the layout will tell you what the card will represent. Keep in mind that the gift may not be tangible—it could be love, health, knowledge, wisdom, or peace of mind—but whatever it may be, it should be accepted or given graciously. It will bring happiness in direct proportion to the manner in which it is given or received.

Special Significance

If the eight of hearts lies in the center of a spread, it indicates an exchange of gifts. The attitude in which the gift is received is as important as the voluntary whole hearted giving of it. The gift may be symbolic or it may link the giver and receiver in an enriching, satisfying intimacy.

When the eight of hearts lies in the top left-hand corner, the client will receive a gift which has deep significance. If the client declines this gift, or accepts it carelessly, it may be a regrettable decision, for this gift could well be the precursor of many other good things waiting to be given. If the eight of hearts appears in the bottom left-hand corner, the gift itself is probably of value, or may come from a source with whom the client has had only a superficial contact.

If the eight of hearts is found in the top right-hand corner, the client will give a gift to someone else. If the act of giving takes place openly and freely, and without expectation of some material advantage, the client will experience considerable spiritual satisfaction. If, on the contrary, the client is driven by less noble motives, the gift may backfire. It should be mentioned that when the eight of hearts is badly placed in a spread, it shows that there is some talk of bribery. Any bribe should be refused at this time.

If the eight of hearts is in the bottom right-hand corner, it indicates that the client will be able to help or serve a stranger. By giving this help or service, the client stands to reap benefits later on.

♥ ♥ ♥

HEARTS: love, self-sacrifice,
  service
NINE: desire, the grand
  passion, philanthropy
NINE OF HEARTS: physical
  pleasure

NINE OF HEARTS

Positive: happiness, pleasure and physical contentment, temporary successes

Negative: vanity, egoism, conceit, self-indulgence

Personal Characteristics

This card is traditionally considered to be the "wish card." In a personal sense, the nine of hearts symbolizes a need for love and affection, as well as a need for money or property. The nine attempts to obtain money for personal use and is seldom rewarded by great success. There will always be money—sometimes a lot of it—but the nine can never count on it!

The same applies to personal relationships. They are present, and have great value, but still don't satisfy the nine. The nine of hearts is not satisfied by personal possessions, nor by relationships. This card must find happiness where it is least expected—and where it is seldom looked for—within the self. It is important that a sense of values be developed, even though those values are developed by trial, error, and a bit of pain.

Since the nine is very helpful to others, this is a person who becomes passionately involved in unsuccessful projects. The nine has difficulty discriminating between worthwhile and futile endeavors, wasting energy and paying the price by feeling inwardly empty and outwardly lonely. The nine represents a tolerant person, capable of sacrificing for ideals. This person tolerates life with its ups and downs, practicing a "love thy neighbor" philosophy. The nine is a philanthropic soul who lives passionately but not always wisely.

The Card

The nine of hearts symbolizes happiness which surpasses all expectations. If the client has expressed a wish, the card indicates that it will be fulfilled, but not in the way the client expects it to be. In many ways, the nine of hearts is the most auspicious card in the deck. It represents spiritual prosperity and development, contemplation, self-knowledge, or affiliation with the life-giving powers of nature. The nine also suggests that riches will remain unattainable if the client doesn't strive to develop wisdom along with other things. Happiness is rendered impossible by greed, avarice, revenge, envy or an immoderate concern for material matters.

Special Significance

If the nine of diamonds appears in the same spread as the nine of hearts, it indicates that plans will probably be successful if they have been pursued wholeheartedly. The combination indicates that a balance between spiritual security, tranquility, self-respect and affluence, public recognition or fame exists for the client.

If a picture card lies next to the nine of hearts, joy will come about because of another person, or another person will share in it. If the nine of hearts and the picture card are separated by the three of diamonds, some element of jealousy is present. The client will have to be careful not to offend others when the three of diamonds falls here.

If the nine of hearts appears in a layout dominated by spades, the client will be able to attain some spiritual growth, firmness of character, maturity or wisdom, in spite of difficulties that may be present. In this case, the nine of hearts is a symbol of a victory which gives the client enough moral strength to develop the personality. It also gives the wherewithal to overcome setbacks. The nine of hearts is symbolic of a key that opens many doors. It is the key to self-awareness and it guides us to rise above circumstances to realize happiness in our own integrity.

HEARTS: love, self-sacrifice,
    service
TEN: success, completion
TEN OF HEARTS: indepen-
    dence in relationships

TEN OF HEARTS

Positive: goals are reached, balance is achieved, success and harmony is attained; peacemaking, generous, cheerful, optimistic; unexpected strokes of good luck

Negative: temptation, stagnation, neglect, carelessness, deterioration, suffering

Personal Characteristics

This card represents a person who has attained a maturity and independence which allows the maintenance of relationships without being attached to them. The tasks set by life can be solved with dedication and care if enough self-confidence is developed to override the opinions of others. This does not mean that the ten isn't a warm-hearted person. Actually the ten of hearts is very responsive to and caring about the partner. The ten expects everyone to approach a relationship the way the ten does; as a base to pursue self-development. A ten of hearts looks to lovers for tenderness and harmony until sated, then the ten moves back out into the world. Relationships are ended when their purpose is done or they are no longer fruitful, usually with the partner's consent. This card may not experience a grand passion, but neither is it haunted by the emotional crises that can attend the end of a love affair.

Driven by creativity and curiosity, and going to great lengths to insure tranquility and harmony, the ten of hearts is not really as sensible as one might think. This individual can be overly emotional when first presented with a problem, although logic usually wins out. Luck is a constant companion, and the ten has the intelligence to both recognize and seize opportunities which come along.

The Card

The ten of hearts represents a messenger who brings good news (usually), but the news is so unexpected that the existing order of affairs is totally upset, and plans crumble. The card is one of optimism and stimulation, although both may be of a temporary nature. Thus, risks should be taken cautiously and infrequently.

Special Significance

More information about the nature of the news brought by the ten of hearts is furnished by the neighboring cards in the spread. A king or queen on either side of the ten indicates that old friends will appear in the near future. A jack or an eight indicates a meeting with young people, or making new contacts. Diamonds signify news concerning money, while a predominance of hearts in a spread indicate an event—such as a marriage, birth of a child, or grandchildren, if the reading concerns an older person.

If the two or ten of spades precede the ten of hearts, it means that the good news will follow some bad news. A situation which looked bleak will end happily. However, if the ten of spades follows the ten of hearts, the good news might turn out to be a mistake. If the two of spades is near the ten of hearts, it indicates that a small misunderstanding or a slight disappointment will follow the good news.

♥ ♥ ♥

HEARTS: love, self-sacrifice,
    service
JACK: idealism, youth
JACK OF HEARTS: a seducer, a
    trickster

JACK OF HEARTS

Positive: friendly, jovial, cheerful, caring, attractive

Negative: a young man, who, in an inscrutable, cunning and subtle way, disturbs and undermines. An intense, impassioned, aggressive character, masked by a peaceful and calm exterior. May be driven by aspirations to power, knowledge, or the realization of personal objectives. Possessed by an all-consuming vanity and ambition. Malicious, ruthless, calculating, unscrupulous and merciless.

Personal Characteristics

Great sacrifice will be asked of the person symbolized by the jack of hearts—especially in early youth—sacrifice in regard to love, affection, education or possessions. When older, the jack dares to give greater rein to personal feelings and will try to understand what affection truly means. This is not easy for the jack of hearts, for this card is suited better to short, but intense contacts.

In order to feel important, the jack may take on the cares of the world—including those of father, mother, brother, sister, the dog or cat, or anyone else. The jack will stay busy arranging everything—trying to straighten out the mess. In general, the jack's compulsion for service will cause estrangement or alienation because the involvement is seen by others as "killing with love."

In reality, the jack of hearts is a responsive figure whose dynamism attracts others like a magnet. He initially approaches everyone in a friendly, hearty, inoffensive manner. He loves pleasure, variety, sexual experience. He tends to evaluate others in terms of their capacity to take care of his needs. Those who lose their heart to a jack of hearts—and many do—may also discover that he can undermine, disturb and manipulate them in order to get his own way. Should all not go well, he may seek refuge in the bottle, trying to evoke all the sympathy he can until a new conquest catches his eye. He seems very susceptible to outside opinions and influences, but the jack only considers others' ideas if they happen to suit his purpose or further his objectives. It is almost as impossible to change his attitude as it is to change the jack of diamonds.

The jack of hearts is so elusive that he intimidates his fellow men, and the enigmatic impression he makes on others often creates distrust. He rarely respects anyone else as he is principally interested in satisfying number one—himself. He feels little responsibility for others and is not above using people for as long as it suits him.

The Card

Where the jack of hearts appears, the client can expect a carefree interlude between more serious periods in life. It can signify an amorous adventure, a marvelous holiday, a special friendship, a party, or some other kind of light interruption of the daily routine. The jack of hearts is both a romantic card and one indicating potential for the foolish reckless pursuit of pleasure.

Special Significance

If the jack of hearts is facing spades, especially the ten or the seven, it indicates that disappointment and heartache will follow overindulgence in merely sensual pleasures.

The jack of hearts in the middle of a spread should be interpreted as a warning to the client—life should be taken more seriously than it is. The jack of hearts is easily given to overeating or drinking, and is inclined to self-indulgence. Fun is one thing—overindulgence is another.

If the jack of hearts appears as the inside card in any of the corners, the client will probably meet someone whose high spirits attract and disarm. The contact could be very agreeable, stimulating and even valuable—but it should not be taken too seriously. If the contact in question is a romantic one, it should be taken lightly because the jack of hearts is often here today and gone tomorrow. If the jack of hearts appears as the outside card in any of the corners, the client can expect a pleasant reward for hard work done in the past.

♥ ♥ ♥

HEARTS: love, self-sacrifice,
    service
QUEEN: reacting, judging
QUEEN OF HEARTS: magnetic
    attraction, reflection

QUEEN OF HEARTS

Positive: a woman who reflects the character of the one who observes her; dreamy, calm, poetic and full of imagination; friendly but without intention of going to great pains on another's behalf; very susceptible to outside influences and therefore more dependent than most other cards—whether in a good or bad position.

Negative: loud, self-indulgent, self-pitying, overly fond of pleasure, melodramatic, frivolous, egotistical, intense

Personal Characteristics

Apart from her almost irresistible charm, the most striking characteristic of a person represented by the queen of hearts is a tranquil sense of preoccupation. She appears to live in a poetic, imaginative world of ecstasy and illusion.

She is a woman who reflects the character of the one who observes her. She is the perfect, patient go-between, ready to receive and pass on the most divergent information, without becoming personally involved. She blurs and undermines every-things solid, certain and firm. She is dependent on others to supply these qualities in her life. Although her personal performance is not always noticable, her helpfulness can hardly be surpassed. One could say that this type of person has no characteristics of her own—but that would be ignoring the concept that openness and permeability also constitute person-ality.

The queen of hearts possesses an all-embracing purity, infinite subtlety and an exceptional sense of beauty. Knowing her is near impossible, as she reflects others and not herself. When the queen of hearts is negatively influenced, these qualities deteriorate. Everything which is received or passed on will be distorted. The negative type may also reap satisfaction from challenging others, from attracting and seducing them to further her own popularity, for she can be intense, instinctive, voluptuous, dramatic and theatrical.

The constructive queen of hearts symbolizes the ideal woman—gentle, maternal mother, the dear sister, or the beloved daughter—tender and full of devotion. She is extremely mild, just, honest, hospitable and candid.

She loves beautiful clothes, the good things in life—but she also needs peace and harmony. She is friendly and convivial, able to entertain people from the most divergent backgrounds and nationalities. She is extremely tolerant of other people's customs, ideals and methods. Since social contacts are her medium, she shouldn't live alone.

The Card

The queen of hearts gives joy, happiness and a love which is neither calculating nor demanding. Her emotional life is rich and deep; her actions are prompted by instinct rather than by reason. According to tradition, she is lighthearted, frivolous and happy. Although she is seldom interested in formal education, she is an inexhaustible source of ideas and inspires talented people around her.

She is attuned to the mental state of those lucky enough to win her love. Through her unwavering faith in their ability, she moves others to carry out their boldest plans and highest aspirations. Although she herself has little creative ability, she feels strongly attracted to art and admires beauty in every form. Her judgment may not always be sound, but she is neither fainthearted nor smallminded.

Friendliness meets with an immediate response on her part, although she is quick to take offense. Though not aggressive or self-interested, she will defend everyone dear to her with great moral courage and physical endurance. She can create a pleasant domestic atmosphere, being an excellent cook and a caring mother; but behind this facade is a life brimming over with fantasy and burning ambition concerning those close to her.

Her cheerfulness has an undertone of melancholy which she seldom reveals. She is sensitive to the suffering of others and the imperfection of life. She stands up for the weak, pities the lonely and fights for justice, but she is easily taken in because she tends to overestimate people. She will hear nothing said against those who are dear to her, but her own candor makes her an easy prey for two-faced people. Her honesty is sometimes tactless and she is capable of intense anger, but she rarely holds a grudge as resentment is really foreign to her nature. She is easily amused and always ready for a chat. She likes company and needs little coaxing in order to enjoy herself. Small marks of attention mean a great deal to her and cordiality can move her. Her favorite pastime is giving pleasure to those in her family and circle of friends.

Special Significance

If a diamond appears to the right of the queen of hearts, the client should be especially wary in regard to financial matters. The ten of hearts to the right of the queen indicates that she will find intense happiness with someone young, probably a child with whom she already has a particularly strong personal tie. If the client is young, the queen's appearance may herald a satisfying love.

If a female client has the queen of hearts in the center of a spread, she will possess many of the characteristics of this card. If the other cards indicate trial, deceit or danger, she is warned to be careful, and not to rely too much on a friendly face or attractive appearance.

If the client is a man and the queen of hearts lies in the middle of the spread, it means that he is the object of a deep love which may come from an entire family. If the queen is in the top right or left-hand corner of the spread, there is a chance of great happiness in the near future. If the queen lies in one of the bottom corners, he will meet a woman who will be a great support to him.

♥   ♥   ♥

HEARTS: love, self-sacrifice, service
KING: vitality, authority
KING OF HEARTS: paternal love

KING OF HEARTS

Positive: a passive, charming, friendly man; quick to anger, yet enthusiastic about people and things; very sensitive, approachable

Negative: indolent, self-indulgent, sensual, melancholy, lazy, dishonest, addictive, self-satisfied

Personal Characteristics

The king of hearts symbolizes a man who is passive, amiable, long-suffering, calm, composed person, who often primarily appears to others as a safe harbor. People who feel oppressed come to him for advice and protection. Since he generally wanders through life in an easygoing manner, the king of hearts seldom has problems in respect to himself. His problems are caused by others or by circumstances around him.

People feel drawn to his warm, good nature and the king of hearts reacts enthusiastically to the attention paid to him. However, his interest diminishes as quickly as it arises. His moods change quickly and this king is quick-tempered as well as changeable. He is soon over the fits of temper because he is not resentful, but he is unable to listen to reason when angry. Nevertheless, he strives for peace and tranquility in his home and environment. His quarrelsomeness is usually an indication that something deeper is at work. It is difficult for him to ask for help although he is quite willing to give it when necessary. He does not require thanks for his efforts.

His warm friendliness makes him the center of family, friends, and work. He responds to injustice with the roar and fight of the lion—always willing to forgive those who have wronged him once the battle is done.

The king of hearts is not fond of travelling, but does like to be active with friends and acquaintances. Unfortunately, he is often on the road, but he never goes so far that he cannot return home in case of necessity. He has a spiritual guilelessness, an innocence and purity which are enviable, and these traits are the source of his inner security.

The Card

In a spread, the king of hearts symbolizes a man of unlimited integrity and good will. This man is honest, loyal, but may appear more simple than he is. He hides his feelings— usually behind grumbling—and is not always easy to understand, preferring to show generosity via action rather than words. He sometimes gives the impression that he is insensitive or incapable of understanding more highly-strung people.

Many are misled by the king of hearts' lack of identifiable emotion. He is often much more complicated than he seems. Innocence and trust in others can sometimes play him false in business or financial affairs. The king is particularly suited to education, the law, or some other profession where strict integrity, silence and thoughtful judgment are essential. The king of hearts is seldom truly creative, but rather appreciates beauty and can enjoy natural simplicity. If the client is a woman or a young man, the king of hearts may represent a father figure or symbol of authority—the rock on which their lives are founded. The fact that the king of hearts is usually seen as a more mature man is not so much a question of age as it is of well-considered opinion, tolerance and wisdom.

Special Significance

If the king of hearts lies next to a jack, and the client is a woman, it indicates that she is trying to instill stability of character, courage and a sense of responsibility in a younger man. She therefore possesses some of the laudable qualities of the king of hearts.

The card can also mean that the woman will find an older man who will guide and support her. In all other suits, marriage between the king and queen usually ends in failure, but the king and queen of hearts make an excellent couple. They shower each other with sincere affection and unconditional trust, and even though their understanding of each other may not reach the deepest recesses of the heart, their lives will be filled and enriched by their love.

A male client having the king of hearts in the center of the spread will endeavor to acquire the traits associated with that card—while a female client will probably seek them in a man. The king may symbolize her husband, father, an ardent admirer, or in some cases, a devoted son.

The appearance of the king of hearts in the top left-hand corner indicates the client will come into contact with such a man in the near future. The client has to decide whether or not to use this man's help and devotion, as conditions or obligations may or may not be attached to the offer. Should the king of hearts appear in the top right-hand corner, it suggests that a man will become a strong force in the client's life, but this friendship can only be won by the integrity of the client himself. The king of hearts is not a man who takes offense quickly, but he is relentless in his battle against dishonesty, irresponsibility, or other breaches of his moral code. Should it come to an open confrontation, the king will fight back undaunted, determined, and sometimes with overwhelming force.

When the king appears at the bottom corners of a spread, he is more likely to be a man who temporarily crosses the path of the client, but who acts as a catalyst. He often assumes a position of authority, smoothing the way for social advance, serving as a guide or mentor in domestic or social situations, or lending financial or moral support in difficult circumstances.

SPADES

SPADES: knowledge, desire
    for knowledge, aloofness
ACE: endeavoring, ruling,
    wanting, individuality
ACE OF SPADES: striving for
    knowledge, thinking

ACE OF SPADES

Positive: a great accumulation of energy for good or bad, conquest, victory, activity, a whirling kind of strength, autumn

Negative: power gained through the suffering of others, or through revenge, punishment, afflictions

Personal Characteristics

Apart from an almost insatiable thirst for knowledge, the ace of spades represents a person who has a need to be surrounded by emotional people. Other people are attractive because the ace finds emotion, itself, inexplicable and curious. This card is tremendously inspired by the volatility and force of highly emotional people, whether this concept is conscious or not.

Nevertheless, the ace values personal intelligence more than the emotional outbursts of others. This individual is neither tolerant nor particularly flexible, and as long as this trait isn't realized, the ace is constantly propelled into the primal world of emotion because it is what is needed for growth. Avoiding emotion causes the ace to remain cold, or hard.

When the ace of spades figures strongly in a reading for a woman, it indicates she may go through life as a meddlesome, gossiping, or even adulterous woman, as long as she is unable to make a connection between her head and her heart. When she finds a man who helps her close this gap, she will remain calm and faithful to him for the rest of her life—for he is her personal "Joseph."

If the ace of spades refers to a male, he will be particularly successful in a social sense. The best years of his life are those of middle age, for he remains curious—searching out the meaning of the universe. This attitude reaches its height around age fifty. He will never find the answers he seeks in existing philosophies or religions, and he may be rather suspicious of vague, overly ethical, or idealistic movements. He must find his own way, all the while keeping his feet firmly on the ground and himself in good health.

The Card

Usually the ace of spades is thought to portend adversity or death. This is not so. The ace of spades represents accumulated strength, power and might. Whether this strength brings about salvation or destruction depends on the actions of the person for whom you read.

Understanding the nature of this strength depends on the card's position. Great things are possible with the ace of spades. If the client is a strong figure, a check can be consciously placed on this energy, and it can be used to conquer many difficulties on the path while facing the future fearlessly. There is some danger, however, concealed in the ace of spades. When it appears, the reader should try to determine its nature and advise the client in regard to exercising self-control. Caution and self-control are both necessary in order to make the most effective use of the energy symbolized by this card.

Special Significance

If the ace of spades appears in the middle of a spread, the client's life will be characterized by strength. The client has the power to heal, and may be a gifted doctor, nurse or other health professional. A capacity for leadership can also make a success-ful lawyer or politician. Your client may excel in any profession where dynamic energy is required.

On the other hand, this person may be capable of consider-able one-sidedness, prejudice or dogmatism. The card symbolizes a need to learn that other people have a right to an opinion of their own. Control will need to be exercised over a bad temper or a compulsion to assert oneself indiscriminantly, since the power of this card may be misused, and by so doing, cause people to unnecessarily turn against your client.

The ace of spades in the top right-hand corner of a spread indicates the existence of power outside the client—a power which must be confronted and turned to the client's purpose. If this energy is handled successfully, your client will emerge from the fray with more authority and self-confidence.

If the ace of spades lies in the top left-hand corner, the client can choose between acknowledging personal power or avoiding it. In this case, you must ascertain to what extent your client can handle new situations. If the client is nearing a crossroads in life, a decision may need to be made. If this person is shy, timid, uncertain by nature, the client should be advised against radical decisions. If the client is courageous, self-assured and adventurous, a risky decision may bring wonderful opportunities. The client always has the last word: the risks should be considered and a decision must be made in regard to taking a path that may be both interesting and difficult.

When the ace of spades appears in the bottom row, the client has an opportunity available, and the neighboring cards will indicate the nature of that opportunity. The client may need to prepare for an emotional storm, an unexpected emergency or a bitter fight with someone who wishes to be the boss. Success with the particular enterprises indicated by the cards will make a considerable improvement in the whole situation.

The ace of spades symbolizes a vital and powerful force that is not by definition dangerous. Whoever uses it correctly will reap an amazingly rich spiritual fruit.

♠ ♠ ♠

SPADES: knowledge, desire for knowledge, aloofness
TWO: being together, going together, working together
TWO OF SPADES: manipulating others, intrigue

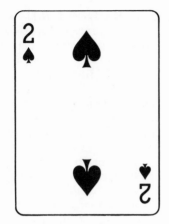

TWO OF SPADES

Positive: peace and quiet, intellect integrated with affections, chastity and silence, honesty, unselfishness

Negative: tension, contradictions, sacrifices and difficulties, dishonesty, indecisiveness, selfishness

Personal Characteristics

The two of spades could be called a card of fear. It suggests some deep-rooted anxiety about the unknown. It represents a person who is not at ease until things have been organized into a philosophical or psychological framework that alleviates anxiety. The two feels threatened by everything, including self, and the slightest provocation elicits a defensive, aggressive response. This person is impulsive, hotheaded and quick to draw conclusions. Having a ready tongue, occasions often give rise to discussions where the opposing point of view is taken with excitement and impatience. Drawing out an opponent, or cleverly maneuvering the debate until the original argument is lost, is fun for the two of spades. It looks as though the two maliciously uses imcomprehension, misunderstanding, and confusion as a smokescreen to disarm an opponent. A form of premeditation must be assumed because the two of spades must know how other people are being handled.

The two works in secret and has the gift of ferreting out hidden information. This card is often found in the secret service, the police department, or in politics. At worst, this individual will act unscrupulously and use cunningly acquired information as blackmail. The two of spades mistrusts all good intentions, and that is one of the reasons why facts are misinterpreted. The two may see other people as objects to be thrown away or replaced when they show signs of wear.

The bottom line is that the two does not trust himself. Perhaps the two of spades is afraid of the consequences of honesty and innocence, since the latter demands surrender and trust. These qualities are alien to the two. Although there is a need to learn cooperation with others (more than any of the other twos), cooperation is often seen as a limitation of freedom.

All of these unattractive characteristics can be reduced to an original "fear of life." As a child, skillful maneuvering may have been necessary to avoid parents' displeasure. In the process, learning to conceal feelings or memories of pain may have caused the development of characteristics that on the surface are charming, but underneath are actually cunning, calculating and vain.

The two eventually marries quite suddenly, and often divorces as quickly. Once past age forty, the need to dominate diminishes somewhat, and available energy can be devoted to a hobby, or philosophical or esoteric pursuits.

The Card

The two of spades is a card of sudden decision concerning a matter of minor importance. Whether the decision is made by your client or someone influential depends on the position of the card in the spread. In both cases, the decision is (or appears to be) prompted by revenge, spite or vexation, rather than by any well-considered.

Special Significance

If the two of spades lies opposite a picture card, the client may be the victim of slander or insinuation. Even though justifiably grieved or irritated, it would be better to maintain self-control. Avoid responding to injustices with angry denials, accusations, threats or tears. The best advice is to leave the matter alone until it can be faced objectively. At that time a better decision can be made.

The client should be warned that the two of spades represents a test of how to cope with unpleasant experiences. If the test is passed successfully, social advance, improvement of personal relationships, or increasing respect from colleagues will occur. In spite of the difficult times it portends, the two of spades can turn out to be a salutary card.

No matter where the two of spades appears in a spread, it always signifies encouragement to continue investigating the situation under discussion. You should discuss the problem in general terms in order to give your client the spiritual peace and fortitude needed to deal with humiliation or opposition. Otherwise the client may lose balance or perspective.

If the two of spades lies in the middle of the spread, the client should be advised not to allow perceptions to be clouded by personal animosity. Overreacting to minor irritations could spoil the success of projects in the long run.

♠   ♠   ♠

SPADES: knowledge, desire
    for knowledge, aloofness
THREE: uncertainty, personal
    development
THREE OF SPADES: indecision,
    passive resistance

THREE OF SPADES

Positive: responsible, dependable, trustworthy in matters of finance

Negative: sorrow, melancholy, unhappy, afraid, interfering, rebellious, sowing discord, causing quarrels, delaying, absence, divorce, deceit

Personal Characteristics

"Seeing is believing" is the motto of the three of spades. The card signifies a person who is a real "doubting Thomas." The three is hard-pressed to believe in the stability of relationships or financial position. This attitude is largely self-fulfilling, and as a result, the three of spades may drift from one job to the next, may have one relationship after another, or change opinions like a chameleon changes color.

It is obvious that the three of spades tries to hold on tight—with both hands—to whatever is believed, possessed or cherished. The three is not really open to innovation, is often intolerant of new ideas, or is mortally afraid of the unknown. This person can also quite easily admit to being wrong if mistakes have been made, and will try once more in a different way—but does not have the slightest faith in that new start! Stubborn, irritated and scornful, the three sits on a fence in such cases, fearing that the next try will also fail—thereby undermining self-confidence once again. If decisions could be made slowly and in a well-considered fashion, without dismissing innovations in advance, the three would soon see that change underlies progress and that by holding tight to the old and the well-known, the development of potential is prevented. This person will encounter difficulties and setbacks in regard to the payment of debts or receiving rightful dues or payments. The three of spades also has potential for physical accidents.

The Card

The three of spades represents a small stumbling block, one which is probably no more than an insignificant annoyance. However, the fact that this card appears in a layout is not without importance. Minor disturbances are easily solved with forebearance and a sense of humor, but when impatience opens the door to anger, stubbornness or revenge, the originally insignificant incidents may assume unreasonable proportions and even ruin carefully laid plans.

Special Significance

If the three of spades occupies a central position, a stumbling block is likely to appear in the near future. Though minor at first, this block will have important ramifications for the client's future. The client should be advised of the danger which might be present, so that he or she can clear away the stumbling block under discussion or avoid it completely. Kindness, consideration, and sober assessment of the difficulty are the best strategies for dealing successfully with problems brought about by the presence of the three.

SPADES: knowledge, desire
    for knowledge, aloofness
FOUR: structure and building
FOUR OF SPADES: spiritual
    stability

FOUR OF SPADES

Positive: truce, peace after war, tranquility after sorrow, relaxation after anxiety, recovery after illness, change for the better, intellectual insight

Negative: uncertainty, stubbornness, egoism, depression

Personal Characteristics

The person represented by the four of spades makes a calm, well-balanced impression on others initially, but upon closer observation it appears that this may be a facade for a considerable amount of uncertainty. The four feels unable to deal with situations which require quick decisions, although this self-doubt is seldom revealed to others.

The four of spades may signify an industrious and superficially well-rounded person who values intellectual flexibility and creativity, while using both to maintain stability. Even though capacity and skills grow, self-doubt continues as a feeling of vague discomfort. The four of spades can even make a virtue out of doubtfulness, and may be heard uttering cries of "Uncertainty is the source of activity and creativity," or somewhat more arrogantly, "Certainty is for the stupid." This emphasis on the intrinsic value of doubt actually begins to constitute a form of self-sufficiency, and the four of spades, in all likelihood, will become a master of some profession as a result.

This person tends to reject any ideas not personally thought of first, and usually rejects changes and innovations that are recommended by others. On closer investigation, the four will reconsider others' suggestions, but with a necessary reserve. Nevertheless, fundamental emotional values or principles are not abandoned for the sake of change, and the four continues to persevere in personal beliefs that relate to right and wrong, good and evil.

Since the four is aware that good working relationships produce far better results than bad ones, because problems can be more easily dealt with, colleagues and employees are given room to be what they are. Little escapes a four in regard to human relationships, and for the most part, perspectives are clear. If fundamental values are challenged by a colleague's behavior, the four will withdraw until personal inner balance is restored.

Carelessness, impurity, pretentiousness, deliberate misinformation, are all considered unattractive traits so every minute spent coping with people exhibiting these traits is considered as time lost. As a result, the four of spades does not have an extensive social life, for social superficiality brings no satisfaction.

During melancholy periods of life, the four of spades may overindulge in alcohol. In general, however, this is a serious, well-balanced person with great reserves of strength.

The Card

The four of spades is a card of recovery or healing. It suggests an end to a long period of illness, anxiety or immoderate tension is in sight. From a superficial point of view, this may be a period when your client is wasting energy. In reality, it indicates a meaningful pause in which new strength is acquired on a physical level, and indicates a "sick leave" from which your client will emerge reborn.

In a spiritual sense, it indicates the end of doubt, indecision and worry. Silence and tranquility will bear the fruit in the shape of new plans, new certainty, deeper insights, and a general enrichment of life.

♠ ♠ ♠

SPADES: knowledge, desire for knowledge, aloofness
FIVE: discord, restlessness, change
FIVE OF SPADES: separation, loss

FIVE OF SPADES

Positive: wide range of experience, energy, intelligence

Negative: dejection, malice, jealousy, slander, weakness, failure, anxiety, poverty, loss (either of honor or good name), sadness following pain or loss, difficulties, lies, distance between friends, a busybody, cruel or cowardly, gossipy

Personal Characteristics

The five of spades represents a person who may be emotionally unstable. The lack of equilibrium may come particurly to the fore in relationships. When any sign of commitment rears its head, the five's freedom is threatened. This person may feverishly seek a way to prevent this loss of freedom, usually hurting the person causing the discomfort.

The five of spades is often a person who is so totally self-engulfed, that the result is a person who drifts. There is an innate restlessness that is never satisfied—and this individual may travel a lot as a result. The five meets or creates difficulties and troubles, never quite understanding why. When the pain is felt, the five leaves—taking flight and leaving ruins behind. The fives' normal impulse to leave when life gets unpleasant, a refusal to make responsible plans, or to estimate what an enterprise will cost, is an eventual cause of difficulty.

To add to this already difficult personality, the five of spades is extremely egocentric, believing in a tremendous sense of personal uniqueness. Practicality, and the rules that others live by have no place in this person's life. The five follows a personal search, and feels the innocent victim of a hostile world. No one will let poor five win.

Because of fickleness—the product of immaturity and a lack of personal responsibility—the five is rarely suited for marriage. At heart, the five longs for marriage and sometimes risks an experiment with it. However, jealousy, suspicion and emotional instability threaten any chance of success. These marriage experiments frequently end in divorce.

The five of spades rarely remains in the birthplace, seldom attends the same school for long, hardly ever finished a course of study, and is incapable of remaining in the same profession for a lifetime. If it happens that the five inadvertantly remains in one business, such radical changes are made in that business that it is no longer recognizable. The five of spades is capable of intelligence and sensibility, but effective use of these traits has to be developed.

The Card

The five of spades is a card of separation. If it appears in the middle of a spread, it usually means that the client will break old ties, change employment, move to a new environment, or undertake a distant journey. Heartache, sorrow, and occasional remorse are inherent in the meaning of the five of spades. This card is traditionally associated with loss, but in most cases loss results from the change that is freely chosen. The sorrow brought about by separation from old friends can be compensated for by new acquaintances, new experiences, and a more satisfying life.

The "separation" may also occur on a mental plane. Old points of view may be abandoned, opinions changed, prejudices eliminated. Beliefs held for years can be thrown overboard or illusions given up.

The five of spades is undoubtedly a difficult card, but certainly not a disastrous one. At its worst, it indicates a loss of friends through violent difference of opinion, abuse or anger. In such circumstances it is preferable to sever all ties rather than prolonging a situation which is characterized by petty bickering, teasing, faultfinding and all the other things people can think of to make life miserable for each other.

Since radical changes and leave-taking from friends, family or work are always coupled with unforeseeable good or bad opportunities, the reader is advised to refrain from definitive recommendations. Your advice should merely help the client along the path to self-knowledge so that irrevocable steps are not taken without first maturely considering the motives.

Special Significance

The cards surrounding the five of spades indicate the nature of the separation, and suggest whether the client will reap joy or sorrow from it. If a separation has been caused by a quarrel, bitterness, or a desire for profit, you could ask your client to reconsider those plans rather than starting a new project too hastily. The separation can probably take place with a minimum of suffering and resentment if your client doesn't overreact to a situation that is viewed as totally intolerable.

If the five of spades appears in the top right-hand corner of a spread, it often indicates that someone from the client's immediate social or professional circle will disappear, or that a long-term situation will undergo a change. When the five of spades is flanked by diamonds, the cause for the separation may be linked to a business reorganization. If the five of spades lies in the top left-hand corner, the separation may not take place at all. The other cards in the corner will suggest the best way to approach the issue in case your client has to make a decision.

Should the five of spades appear in the bottom corners, the separation will accompany other events. A person or situation will disappear, and is only important insofar as the job, financial or social position may be adversely affected.

♠ ♠ ♠

SPADES: knowledge, desire
for knowledge, aloofness
SIX: mediation, adaptation,
understanding of life
SIX OF SPADES: solicitude,
responsibility

SIX OF SPADES

Positive: knowledge, intelligence which has proven socially useful, success following problems, sensitivity, travel by air

Negative: selfishness, arrogance, egoism, intellectual pride

Personal Characteristics

This is a card which points to future tensions. The six of spades reacts quickly to personal intuition. This is an individual who is either carefree, careless and lazy, or one who is hardworking—a productive avant-gardist. There appears to be no middle ground as this is an individual of extremes. The six is free to determine how to use great sensitivity and sharp intelligence. These gifts can be developed into valuable, finely-honed instruments, or they can be wasted on trifles.

The life of the six of spades goes in cycles. During one period, life may go very well and then fortune takes a turn for the worse and things don't go so well. Then the cycle starts all over again. The six can learn to accept this phenomena as a logical personal sequence, and the experience can be interpreted as the greatest possible opportunity for developing potential gifts to the fullest. The peace of mind acquired through insight into this life cycle process is very important, for it brings a more tolerant attitude toward the needs of others.

The six of spades approaches work with an inexhaustible patience, calm, industry and capability. This is not a person who needs the limelight. Work and self-discipline are in the blood, automatically bringing the six to a desired position. All this notwithstanding, a six of spades may devote more thought to the wishes of others than to personal interests. It is not that personal interests are denied, but they are not pursued at the expense of other people.

This person is even-tempered and capable of overcoming almost all adversity because of a basic understanding of life principles and cycles. The six doesn't always do what is best, and learns that too much emotion or intrigue will bring vulnerability and general unhappiness. When this happens, the six becomes nervous, uncertain or worried. For this reason, the six is called the anxiety card.

The Card

The six of spades is a card of anxiety in a reading. It often indicates a period of tension that the client has to wait out. The client (or someone close) may be ill, but the card usually indicates a time when welfare depends on other people's decisions. The client may feel threatened, or confined, or discouraged in regard to taking steps for personal reasons. You could determine whether this difficult period will have an unfavorable or a favorable outcome by looking at the cards surrounding the six. Because the outcome of the reading is not always "in the cards" it might be wise to discuss the problem as the client sees it, also preparing your client for a change in attitude about how the problem is perceived. Not everything that looks bad is actually so. Anxiety should be put aside while time is spent immersed in other activities because a better decision can be made in regard to the situation at a later time. This card may even be used to build success if the energy is handled wisely.

♠ ♠ ♠

SPADES: knowledge, desire
for knowledge, aloofness
SEVEN: insight, a turning
point
SEVEN OF SPADES: sudden
insight, reversal

SEVEN OF SPADES

Positive: perseverance, independence, introspection, conscientiousness

Negative: lack of balance, vain endeavors against too powerful resistance, partial success through giving up the fight just before victory, lack of staying power, aimlessness, uselessness, futility, hypernervousness, untrustworthiness, disorganization, dishonesty

Personal Characteristics

This card describes a person who lives by the grace of "great" inspiration. If this inspiration is not realized consciously, or it is absent for a time, the seven of spades drifts aimlessly around and worries about all kinds of things which never happen. The motto for this card could be "Live according to your insights; trust them but be prepared to pay for them." The seven of spades can always earn a living if that is desired, but just as the seven mistrusts personal flashes of inspiration, the seven likewise views any personal value to society with suspicion.

The financial position of any seven is frequently not too rosy, so the seven panics about money. This individual can invest money in useless speculative ventures which cause even more financial problems. The seven can also be secretive about financial status in general, sometimes having more or less than what is discussed with others.

The source of some of the seven's difficulties may be the fact that enterprises or alliances are not carefully thought out before hand. Periods of poverty are inevitable. In order to survive them, the seven has to denote body and soul toward making a regular living. This is done unwillingly, since the seven doesn't want to be a part of the social order and its rules. The seven is sometimes connected with backbiting and scandal. Indeed, if the seven is not purposefully employed, difficulties may be encountered in work or relationships. These may occur because the individual is not trusted or understood by those in the immediate circle—or the seven may really be dishonest. In either case, the result is the same: the seven becomes more nervous, and health is affected adversely.

The seven of spades needs tangible palpable certainties. As soon as the ground is not solid, the seven abandons the project and looks elsewhere for security. This person should be particular about the way work is performed, in order to avoid becoming uncertain, careless, etc., and should also avoid keeping company with those who drink too much, or who have little personal drive. The seven of spades is very comfortable alone because the squabbles of everyday interactions with people is therefore avoided. This card also needs to be alone in order to reinstate feelings of personal self-confidence. Once the inner self is in order, the seven can run back out to join with people for a while. When the seven of spades stands firm, honors the natural intuition available, enjoys a good education, and faces life from a positive point of view, the card will symbolize self-made success.

The Card

The seven of spades is a card of division. The client's plans will only partially succeed. In addition, the card foretells unexpected twists and turns in a career. Wherever the seven of spades appears, the client will discover that success and recognition are not forthcoming. This card indicates that plans should be reevaluated for there are more difficulties ahead than the client is aware of. Perhaps a loss is in order, and that should be prepared for. When this card is present in a spread, small irritations should be avoided, as emotional responses may affect the future plans. As diplomatically as you can, talk to your client about success—and encourage the client to consider success that is won through hard work as the kind of success that is more lasting.

SPADES: knowledge, desire for knowledge, aloofness

EIGHT: power, will, organization

EIGHT OF SPADES: emotional influence

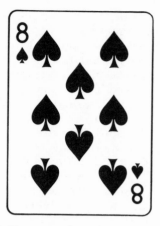

EIGHT OF SPADES

Positive: willpower, talent for organization, good regenerative powers

Negative: interruption, disturbance, obstacles, waste of energy on details at the expense of taking care of important matters, lack of perseverance, unexpected setbacks, limitation, great care negated by carelessness

Personal Characteristics

This card indicates a mixture of power, intuition, sensitivity, and violent emotions. The person ruled by this card needs to learn how to maintain balance in order to avoid chaotic situations, for when chaos is present, the card is open to all kinds of influences—especially on an emotional level. Because the eight is familiar with emotional disturbances in life, keep in mind that this person will also end inadequate emotional alliances—and breaks may take place in either the personal life or in business situations.

The eight of spades is a very strong card, indicating a person who will not be held back by anything or anyone. This person pursues every impulse and heads straight for a goal. The eight considers no mountain too high to climb in pursuit of knowledge needed. The greatest potential is reached when working for large organizations, for this individual unconsciously exerts a considerable influence, and can convince people to work together for the benefit of a group.

When the eight of spades is ill, the source of the illness is usually psychological. This person, fortunately, possesses great regenerative powers, which help in times of stress. The eight will experience the depths and the heights of life, and the experience will encompass physical as well as psychological aspects of life.

The eight is vulnerable to emotional manipulation. If this person wishes to maintain a sense of personal security, the emotional life and emotional responses to other people will have to become more conscious.

The Card

The eight of spades is a card of fulfillment. It represents a safe harbor, a refuge free from earthly cares and tensions. It is a card of tranquil joy and pleasure. The calm contentment it promises may be connected with another person, or with a particular environment, or a favorite occupation. Indications concerning the nature of the beneficial influence will be found in the surrounding cards.

The eight of spades only reflects one aspect of the client's life, however. It is not a total card. The small moments of happiness within the client's reach are but an interlude in the mainstream of everyday activities. If the client wants to hold on to the benefits symbolized by the eight of spades, the benefits must be separated from the rest of the lifestyle. In some way, the client needs to keep active in another sense, to avoid becoming a slave of some desire. In order to determine what this is, you will have to look at the rest of the cards in the spread and discuss the situation with the client.

♠ ♠ ♠

SPADES: knowledge, desire for knowledge, aloofness
NINE: desire, the grand passion, philanthropy
NINE OF SPADES: loss of intelligent control, disturbances, an adventurer

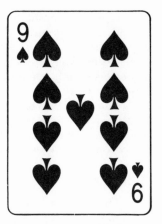

NINE OF SPADES

Positive: obedience, trustworthiness, patience, unselfishness, conscientiousness

Negative: cruelty, fear, doubt, hopelessness, worry, suffering, loss, illness, malice, nitpicking, cunning, lying, scandal-mongering, obsessing

Personal Characteristics

The person described by the nine of spades is someone driven by an insatiable hunger for sensation. On the one hand, the card could be called an irresponsible adventurer, but on the other, the card is capable of fulfilling obligations conscientiously. The nine is extremely curious, and will often find something special to study—becoming impassioned about any field of endeavor chosen. It is possible to say that the nine may waste a lot of time on superficialities, and this will become a source of trouble, for the card needs a serious purpose in life.

In personal relationships, the nine likes a lot of tension, including obsessive or hysterical situations. The nine reacts instinctively and passionately to both people and things, so the domestic life may not be calm. There is a tendency to boredom in long-term relationships, and the nine can end a relationship in what could be considered a cold and detached manner. The people left behind may see the nine as a person of little sensitivity. When counselling this person, keep in mind that the nine is also very upset when the domestic life is not in order!

We could say that the nine of spades symbolizes someone who is not very secure, which means that a considerable amount of approval and sympathy from others is needed. People who surround the nine will exert a great influence, for if the social circle can stimulate the nine's helpful qualities, they will be developed; if the social circle stimulates qualities that are not particularly well devleoped, the nine may end up being banal, coarse or indifferent. In today's world, we might even call this "jaded." The nine's inherent sense of duty needs to be expanded if the nine wants to experience the most from life.

If the nine of spades refers to a female, she will tend to choose a relationship whereupon she is taken care of. She may be willing to lend a hand at the beginning of the relationship, but that will not last long. She may be a sentimental, pleaure-loving person who needs to learn the meaning of reliability. She may be someone who easily commits adultery, or one who is involved in trivia. Deeper relationships are possible for this card, and how to develop relationship potential will be one of her life's issues.

The male nine of spades will also need to determine his life-style. On the one hand, he can play the role of an older, wiser brother, or the fatherly type who stretches out his hand to help younger people. On the other hand, he could be doing this in order to stay in touch with a rather irresponsible and primitive nature. This could be interpreted as the folksaying in Holland, "When the fox preaches, watch your geese." This man could also be someone who is drawn to a motherly type of woman whose philanthropic nature will bring out the same character-istics in him. He may also choose to relate to a woman who is older and financially helpful to him. If he chooses a woman based on her financial security, he may be able to do as he wishes while taking on little in the way of responsibility.

The Card

The nine of spades is a traditional card of good luck. It has also been associated with lightning, the swift strike of angry power, the end of deep-rooted habits of life, or the collapse of the Tower of Babel. This is partly true. The nine does indicate unpredictable changes, but it is also an indicator that the client can clean away a lot of dross to begin anew. It is important that the client be aware that changes are coming, for the danger implied by this card indicates that the destructive old ways will have to be replaced by something new—and the client may not be ready.

The nine of spades is also known as a card representing fear. Fear can always be overcome and it will be up to the reader to open the door for new ways of thinking. For a very young client, the card can indicate that the young person is getting ready to leave home for the first time—and the fear would be related to leaving the parental nest. For the older client, it may indicate some change in the family, or a loss of security, or the insecurity that occurs when a new lifestyle is started.

Special Significance

If the nine of spades carries an important place in the layout, the client should be warned about the need for some kind of reorientation in life. It may be wise for the client to leave the past and redirect the lifestyle into the future. Perhaps the client needs to let go of preconceived notions so new patterns can be developed.

If the nine of spades is present in the center of the spread, it suggests that the client needs to develop a broader outlook, to seek new friends, to adopt a new way of thinking. Breaking old ties may be painful, but we cannot move on to a bright future when we are carrying around an old pack of troubles or habits. If the nine of spades lies to the left side of the spread, the client then has a choice about keeping to the old path or not. The reader can determine more about this situation by looking at the cards that surround the nine.

♠ ♠ ♠

SPADES: knowledge, desire
  for knowledge, aloofness
TEN: success, completion
TEN OF SPADES: disappointment, failure

TEN OF SPADES

Positive: intelligent, a fluent speaker, clear intelligence, subdued gaiety, modest hope

Negative: downfall, destruction, mischief, disaster, failure, separation, the end of false hope, misconceptions, hopeless ideas, irrelevance

Personal Characteristics

The ten of spades is the card of someone who approaches life from an abstract point of view. The card indicates an intelligent, fluent speaker, who has a good sense of humor along with a lifelong interest in the pursuit of education and knowledge. Because of a lack of self-confidence, personal theories may never be tested. This hesitant attitude increases a tendency to hold onto familiar norms. Conservatism in the ten, therefore, may have its origin in a basic mistrust of personal intuition or vision. The ten of spades is not known for its natural intuitive ability, for hunches cannot be blindly acted upon by this card.

A warm, loving domestic environment is of paramount importance to the ten of spades. Great sacrifices may be made to hold onto security. Some tens have a business at home, even though this presents inconveniences and disturbances in the personal life.

Although tens are traditionally considered to be success cards, this is less true for the ten of spades since success will be determined by intellectual maturity. This card may drift until age thirty, scornfully criticizing everything. If the career is not started prior to age thirty, the ten will be behind all those who started to work earlier. The ten does have intellect and business acumen which can bring rewards, particularly in the field of finance. The ten sometimes has a tendency to weigh the pros and cons of an issue to such an extent that it becomes a detrimental time-wasting factor. Fear of the unfamiliar may prevent the necessary growth that will bring maximum yields from natural abilities.

The ten must also cope with confusion and uncertainty, and these traits may keep the ten involved in the status quo. Too many decisions may be made because of a fear or anxiety about the future. Business may deteriorate, and even the domestic life may suffer because of this tendency. Then the ten cries about a wasted life. When doing a reading for a ten, it would be good to ascertain where this person is on the path, because encouragement to develop natural talents may be needed. Developing self-confidence will be a main issue for this card.

The Card

The ten of spades symbolizes a wall or a barrier of some sort. It can indicate the end of a dream, the unmasking of false aims, or the compulsory renunciation of a long cherished plan. Since it is not easy to accept the end of a particular phase of life, feelings of depression, disappointment, bitterness or humiliation may occur. Under such circumstances, it is easy to bang one's head against the wall, trying to blame others for a turn of events, or sinking into self-commiseration. Acceptance of what is should be the key here. Once the issue is accepted, it can be let go, and a new plan can be developed.

Special Significance

If the ten of spades is the outer card in any corner of the spread, it signifies that a path that once looked promising is leading to a dead end. The client should be urged to revise plans, for another route must be sought in order to extend options. Who knows—maybe the old road might have led to disaster. Seen in this light, the barrier may appear to be a blessing.

If the ten of spades appears in the middle of the layout, it indicates that important news will bring about some reversal in the client's life. Someone as yet unknown may play a decisive role. You can determine whether or not the situation will be beneficial or detrimental by looking at the cards surrounding the ten. All is not lost because a path is blocked. Wisdom and courage may be needed to discover a new direction. Your client may need to consider a change in attitude—especially if the reaction to this information includes a feeling of hopelessness.

♠ ♠ ♠

SPADES: knowledge, desire for knowledge, aloofness
JACK: idealism, youth
JACK OF SPADES: unbalanced seeker, a scornful pedantic type

JACK OF SPADES

Positive: at first sight this person may be a friendly, intelligent young man, full of ideas and plans, whose aims may be vague and whose flexibility may give rise to contradictions

Negative: he destroys as quickly as he creates and constructs, sometimes being hateful, malicious, manipulative, untrustworthy, fanatical, pitiless, cynical

Personal Characteristics

The jack of spades can be considered a memory card for it signifies a person who lives intensely and digests all experience —and never forgets the lessons learned. The jack has a researching mind which takes him to the most improbable places, to the most wonderful nooks and crannies, in search of new experiences. In some ways this card is called the card of the future, for the jack tries to meld the known with the unknown. The jack is often called unconventional because of this interest.

Sometimes it is called ambivalent, because others do not understand what the jack is attempting to do.

The jack of spades wants to be self-assertive, but when he is thwarted in any way, there is a tendency to drown disappointments in alcohol. The card signifies restlessness and inconsistent behavior. The jack can drift from one job to another. This person may have difficulty finding a way to realize ideals, and may also have difficulty committing himself to anything solid. On the one hand, he abhors pettiness and pretentiousness, and on the other, he can be called petty himself, as his behavior is often inconsistent. He spends money like water, causing others to further distrust his stability.

In relationships, the jack has an intense inner life, which causes him to land in unusual relationships. He sometimes causes himself great sorrow and disappointment. There is a need for a totally absorbing life—he is a person difficult to satisfy. He can be intellectual at the wrong times, assuming a neutral, distant, or uninvolved attitude, which doesn't make him popular in relationships. He can be involved in meaningless relationships as well, and a poorly thought out interlude can cause him to lose a relationship of value.

The jack of spades does well if he works in an intellectual atmosphere because mental exertions give him the greatest satisfaction. His intelligence can be used as a weapon against obstacles and disappointments. He sees people as sparring partners in intellectual jousts. However, the jack of spades does hold his small circle of friends in warm regard. They may not believe they can count on the jack, but as far as he is capable, he is loyal to those he cares for.

The Card

The jack of spades signifies a young person and the sex of that person will be determined by the cards around it. If the jack is lying opposite a heart or a club, it signifies someone of the opposite sex than your client. If the jack is the last card in a center spread, look at the suit of the card above it to determine which sex you are looking for. If the jack is the last card in a corner of a spread, and is looking outward, it means that the jack signifies a person who will disappear from the client's life. Whether or not the client will feel badly about this will be determined by the cards nearby.

The jack of spades always represents a young person who is not yet fully mature. Therefore, the character description is not as sharply defined as it would be with cards representing older people. In general, if the card has male connotations, the character of the king of spades will develop. If indications show the card to be a female, the person will be apt to develop into a queen of spades type.

The jack of spades is always a friendly card. If he is a young man, he will be dynamic, quick to react to innovation, bursting with nervous energy. He seeks an outlet in sports or in intellectual research. His abilities are still somewhat in the air—he needs more depth in order to build himself the position he wants in life. He may also waste a great deal of energy on trivia.

If a female client is interested in such a young man, she should ask herself if she is capable of being the stabilizing force in a relationship with him. If she herself is lighthearted, uncertain or quick tempered, the relationship may be characterized by endless quarreling, misery and an eventual breakup. The relationship will only be satisfying and successful if she gets the chance to channel her energy in a direction that will allow a true sense of unity to grow between them. As long as your female client is uncertain, she should not make any final decisions. It is better to think seriously about the future and what you want from it. Although this young man may seem very romantic to her at the moment, he is really very serious and seeks a partner who can help him attain the goal he sets for himself.

If your client is a young man, and the jack of spades represents a young woman in his spread, your client should be prepared for a series of surprises. This young woman may seem outwardly calm, but she is a deeply emotional, ardent, intuitive type, who stands up for her rights. Her personality has many facets, some of which directly oppose each other, and she is therefore hard to understand. She can behave like a spoiled and unpredictable child, but this behavior may mask a strong will which strives for concrete goals. She aims high, enlisting help from others. She is capable of using any ruse to get her way. She also has a warm heart and will defend those she loves through thick and thin. She cannot be conquered by storm, but responds better to a long courtship. The man who wins her can count himself lucky to have such a partner, but he should not expect that all future surprises will be equally pleasant!

SPADES: knowledge, desire
    for knowledge, aloofness
QUEEN: reacting, judging
QUEEN OF SPADES: objective,
    intelligent judgment,
    intuitive powers of ob-
    servation

QUEEN OF SPADES

Positive: an elegant woman, intuitive, strong, wise, calm, digni-
fied, strict, aloof, just, benevolent, subtle, practical

Negative: vengeful, aggressive, cruel, secretive, deceitful, calculating, untrustworthy, a dangerous opponent, superficially
attractive

Personal Characteristics

All four queens in the deck represent a facet of the
receptive principle, and the queen of spades does this via
intelligence. Her judgment is practical, well considered, logical,
and if she expresses an opinion about something, it is an
intellectual rather than an emotional one. Her intuition never
lets her down, not even in the emotional situations which she
generally finds difficult to handle.

This card describes a person whose thirst for knowledge is
insatiable, and who has little patience for the ignorance or
mental laziness of other people. She needs freedom of action,
detests interference by third parties, and often avoids marriage.
Her uncertainty in regard to matters of feeling is caused by an
overly analytical attitude, further strengthening her position in
regard to marriage in general. The queen of spades would not
be described as domestic, but she has a strongly maternal
element that makes her seem strangely aloof, yet warm.
Whenever she suffers on account of something or someone, she
suffers long and deeply. She is neither devoted nor humble, and
never giving up control of herself in any alliance.

She is generous and spends her money as quickly as she earns it. She permits herself this pleasure because her performance is usually exceptional, and provides her with more money than she needs. She possesses a gift of leadership and is best suited to a profession. Trade or general business is not her long suit. Her weak area is her apparent lack of sympathy, for a little more tolerance on her part would bring a better reception to those important to her in business.

All in all, the queen of spades is a creative, inspired, inventive woman, who can see future events before they arrive, and is able to work ahead of her time.

The Card

From a superficial point of view, this card represents a "dark" woman. This has nothing to do with race, nor is it an indication of wickedness, as one so often hears. Still waters run deep, and this describes the queen of spades. The woman symbolized by this card tends to hide her feelings under a mantle of dignity, especially later in life. and she may appear impassive, haughty, cool or unapproachable. This is a difficult woman to gauge, but her friendship is worthwhile seeking. Once she has given it, she remains loyal no matter what lies ahead. On the other hand, she can be implacable, cruel, and a merciless enemy. A woman like this should be confronted openly because she has a sixth sense for deceit and treachery. If one doesn't approach her with an honest motive or a sincere desire for friendship, she will know.

The queen of spades usually has an exceptionally strong and richly lived personal life, but her appearance in a card reading doesn't signify romance. Her role is rather that of a protector, advisor, or confidante. Should a romantic relationship exist between her and your client, she will turn out to be quite a source of surprises—being both passionate and jealous.

Her natural psychic abilities make her receptive to telepathic knowledge, so her advice should be carefully considered. Her powers of discrimination are sharp, her judgement of people is accurate—in so far as she doesn't project anything onto others unnecessarily. Many successful people know a queen of spades, especially those in the field of art. For example, her high standards may provide an artist with structure, stability, inspiration, or she may be the power propelling him toward the top.

Even though the queen may be bossy or aggressive, she is easy to know if you meet her with unaffected friendliness and if you respect her point of view. Once such an emotional attachment has been formed, her noblemindedness and sense of sacrifice knows no bounds, but she can be a very dangerous opponent to anyone who crosses her. She is quick to uncover weakness in an enemy, and can think up the most refined ways of humiliating or tormenting the rascal who has offended her.

Her existence is complex, lending her an aura of mystery and enigma, of incalculable obsession or contradictory caprices. She is a woman who deserves a great deal of attention, but it is difficult to predict whether the attention you give will be received gracefully or simply refused.

♠ ♠ ♠

SPADES: knowledge, desire
    for knowledge, aloofness
KING: vitality, authority
KING OF SPADES: intelligent
    authoritative judgment

KING OF SPADES

Positive: an active, serious, clever man who is also fierce, ambitious, authoratative and unimpeachable

Negative: someone indecisive, deceitful, cunning, tyrannical

Personal Characteristics

The king of spades represents a person who is not easy to get along with. He tends to see things in black and white, and may, even with the best of intentions, tread on someone else's toes. As a manager or supplier, he seldom makes mistakes, and his business insight makes him loved and respected by his colleagues. When measured by his own standard, the king is noblehearted, reasonable and friendly. In the eyes of the opposition he is sometimes the willful tyrant who refuses to see, or who is incapable of appreciating, any point of view but his own. He mistrusts everything which smacks of intuition, and has a crushing opinion of the artistic talents, revolutionary ideas, or fiery enthusiasms of those close to him. This attitude obviously leads to domestic unhappiness, opposition in business affairs, or even the loss of friendship.

Business cares or social problems often blind the king to the finer nuances of different lifestyles. Open opposition and biting criticism will heighten his stubbornness. If you want to have him listen to you, it might be wise to sincerely praise his performance, for then he will listen to an alternate opinion. He is actually quite sentimental, and when his better side is called upon, he rises to the occasion. The king of spades is gifted with a fine intelligence, and thinks in clearcut conceptions, being particularly successful as a merchant, lawyer or engineer. In spite of his outward self-assurance, however, he has a great need for the warm ties of friendship, and he also needs someone to love. He cannot bear loneliness, cherishing any affection shown him, even though he may appear to be indifferent.

The Card

When the king of spades appears in a spread, it indicates the presence of a powerful, authoritative man who is intelligent, highly principled and ambitious. When this card lies in the middle of the spread, the card represents the client himself. Traditionally, the king of spades is portrayed as an older man of dark appearance, a description which is too superficial, because "dark" doesn't refer to the color of the hair, nor does it describe the complexion. It indicates character, masculinity, and an ability to control situations. He doesn't necessarily have to be old: the card is rather an indication that his attitude toward life is mature—or not easily changed. The king does run the risk, however, of blocking his growth in regard to new spiritual or moral values because of his lack of communication. When he chooses to show his good will in a sincere manner, the king is capable of just and fair judgment.

Special Significance

If your client is a female, the king of spades represents a man who plays an important role in her life—be it father, brother, husband, friend, or possible lover. The woman who is considering either a marriage or a business relationship with such a man should thoroughly examine her capabilities and expectations, as this is not a man to be wound round her little finger. Should she count on doing so, she will be quite disappointed. If she is really able to be supportive of this man, giving him the warmth and emotional security he needs, she may be sure that he will care deeply for her the rest of her life.

If the king of spades lies in the center of the spread, your client knows the man well. If the card appears on the right side of the spread, she already knows the man, but the relationship still has little significance to her. If the card is on the left side of the spread, your client will soon meet this man.

◆ ◆ ◆

DIAMONDS

DIAMONDS: possessions, financial affairs, the spirit of enterprise

ACE: endeavoring, ruling, wanting, individuality

ACE OF DIAMONDS: striving for possessions, "I do"

ACE OF DIAMONDS

Positive: strength, work, wealth, materialism in every conceivable form, worldliness, physicality, winter

Negative: uncertainty, greed, quick temper, rigidity, cunning

Personal Characteristics

The ace of diamonds symbolizes a clash between idealistic love and practical values. Love for another person and love of possessions often struggle together for the upper hand. One will win out because the person signified by the ace of diamonds is incapable of managing both. If infatuation changes to love, financial matters are forgotten—or become a problem. The material side usually triumphs. Contact with other people is of paramount importance, although great secrecy may be practiced in respect to relationships, both private and business.

This is a card that indicates gallant behavior, hidden grief, or a life full of pitfalls and emotional shortcomings. Nevertheless, the ace of diamonds does have constructive technical talent which can be used to advantage.

The Card

The ace of diamonds is traditionally considered to represent money, but this view oversimplifies its significance. This ace is a card of magic and witchcraft, and since magic and knowledge were considered the same at the time the cards came into existence, this card also represents mathematical knowledge, or a natural aptitude for astronomy, archeology or architecture.

The old wisdom taught that the foundations of magic lay in the home. The true magician was therefore seen as a "builder of houses" and the ace of diamonds is a card which denotes this constructive power. Throughout the ages, the spiritual wisdom of the magician was gradually replaced by the juggler card, the man who could juggle with skill and who had to know a few tricks to bluff the audience and keep his job. The true magician is a character builder, since the power lies not in practical skills, but in an ability to understand and articulate outside influences. As a conveyor of insight and understanding, the magician has great value.

The ace of diamonds is not a card of easy satisfaction, and luxury, as is sometimes suggested. It symbolizes a perpetually restless spirit with an indefatigable thirst for knowledge. It denotes dissatisfaction with life in its present form, and an interest in bringing great projects to fruition. In its best form, this ace represents an unselfish devotion to progress. At its worst, this is the card of the calculating egoist, a merciless and clever manipulator who can make a financial killing anywhere. You must be cautious when interpreting the ace of diamonds, for the presence of its creative power is a certainty, and it is up to you to indicate how your client can best use the available talent.

The youthful male client should be encouraged to concentrate on the techniques necessary in the practice of a profession, whereas the "magical power" of a female client will apply either to profession or family. Organization is in her blood, even though she may not know it. She can influence others and help with character formation, development of personality, or can be influential in regard to the education of other people. She is a superb teacher or manager, but should value inner achievements as well as her technical skills.

Special Significance

If the ace of diamonds plays a dominant role in a spread, talents can be used for organization. The "house" your client builds may be a business, the reorganization of a department, the merger of several companies, a home, or a better application of some technical skill.

If the ace of diamonds is found in the top left corner of a spread, the client should be on guard. There may be a chance to improve on the job, but the chance may pass by unheeded if it is not looked for.

If the seven, nine or ten of spades lies to the left of the ace of diamonds, it is better to slow down in order to avoid the calamity that may be caused by some hasty action. The appearance of the ace of diamonds in the top right corner means the client has already launched an adventurous plan or will shortly do so. In this case, the other cards should be carefully studied. The two of spades to the left of the ace of diamonds warns of delay. The ten of spades to the right of the ace of diamonds advises the client to look for another method of implementing a plan. If hearts or clubs are lying next to the ace of diamonds, they promise a successful, fruitful end to a plan already in the works.

A peculiar trait of the ace of diamonds is that the power of the card cannot be arrested. The client who makes use of the opportunities signified by the ace will note a change in lifestyle. Opportunities signified by this ace usually contain some financial advantage. If too much emphasis is placed on money, it could be at the expense of more important values which actually lie closer to the heart. Perhaps you should talk to your client about the fact that too much concentration on one particular project may result in other losses.

DIAMONDS: possessions, financial affairs, the spirit of enterprise

TWO: being together, going together, working together

TWO OF DIAMONDS: working together in matters of finance or enterprise

TWO OF DIAMONDS

Positive: changes, alternating profits and losses, strength and weakness, ecstasy and melancholy, health and illness

Negative: changing occupations, drifting, busy but not stable

Personal Characteristics

This card represents both business and service, and suggests that this individual can work exceptionally well with others. The two of diamonds differs from other twos insofar as this person suffers from less anxiety and is prone to fewer ups and downs. The two of diamonds is determined, possesses an infallible sense of intuition, and is able to accurately diagnose people and situations.

The two of diamonds goes its own way. Not easily influenced, and not giving an inch in a discussion, the two stands his or her ground—sometimes too firmly—facing the world with self-assurance. There is a tendency toward complacency, which may lead to unhealthy relationships, ultimately slowing down development. All twos live behind a facade, but the two of diamonds is aware of the mask, why its there and what lies behind that personal facade.

The two of diamonds is a powerful, active and aware person who is drawn to intelligent people. There is some conflict in life, however, for a chronic illness or other handicap may disturb or prevent activities or ambitions. There is a considerable interest in money, as this card has a natural talent for negotiation and business.

The Card

The two of diamonds symbolizes a message concerning money or business. It usually indicates a pleasant, albeit small, surprise. The news may concern a gift, transfer of property, legacy, or a chance of a better position. If spades are involved, the news may bring relief from opposition or disappointment.

Special Significance

If the two of diamonds appears in one of the corners, it describes an event which has no direct link to the client's life. If the card appears in the middle of the spread, the news will have a far-reaching effect which may not be readily apparent. The news will change the client's circumstances in some way, for there will be some new contacts with different people, or money may be used for new ventures.

The cards which surround the two of diamonds will help you advise your client. If the two occupies an important position, it signifies that a relatively small investment on the client's part can bring rewards. Money spent on journeys, education, hobbies, club-membership, or in some way that enlarges the mental outlook will serve to enrich life more than your client will understand at the moment.

◆ ◆ ◆

DIAMONDS: possessions, financial affairs, the spirit of enterprise

THREE: uncertainty, personal development

THREE OF DIAMONDS: uncertainty in matters of finance

THREE OF DIAMONDS

Positive: work, business, paid employment, commercial transactions, constructive building, establishment of a business, easy recovery from failure

Negative: egotistical, limited, prejudiced, greedy, unrealistic, precarious

Personal Characteristics

The three of diamonds represents a person who is caught between two basic views: one materialistic, the other spiritual. If the three of diamonds is working in a strictly materialistic field, this person may prefer to work secretly, or may be uncommunicative or unapproachable. Others know little of decisions beforehand.

The three of diamonds works hard. This card learns from practical experience, and beliefs are difficult to change. The three hangs on to what is known—and this fact could be the three's greatest handicap. In business it can mean that the three is more susceptible to becoming a victim of sudden changes, or this person may be blind to the necessity for quick action.

The three of diamonds needs people with whom opinions can be exchanged. Although this need may be recognized, the three doesn't like to leave home to visit a friend. This can make for difficulties. The three can also draw into a shell, and the inner conflict caused by the two opposing facets of personality can cause obvious personal discomfort from time to time.

It often takes the three of diamonds a long time to understand inner motivations. Although life doesn't run smoothly, the three usually succeeds in expressing or giving form to natural talents. This card indicates that the family causes problems of some sort, and sometimes these problems relate to a son. The marriage doesn't run like clockwork, and the three may marry more than once, because the first marriage may not provide lasting satisfaction. Don't be too surprised if you hear that the three of diamonds ends a marriage rather abruptly, for when the decision to leave is made, the plans are put into action quickly.

The Card

The three of diamonds in a reading will often represent a legal document, such as a contract, will, tenancy agreement, or papers connected with buying or selling goods. Occasionally, this card symbolizes a dispute about financial matters where legal documents are not appropriate. It could also denote legal contracts that are not directly concerned with money, such as marriage, divorce, adoption, custody or the like. The three of diamonds indicates financial or legal developments, but gives no clear indication of the result of the activity.

Special Significance

The card lying immediately above the three of diamonds can tell you more about the results of any legal matters. If the five of diamonds is above the three, it suggests some kind of bitterness. The seven of diamonds indicates a solution to difficulties, which will be of great help to your client. The nine of diamonds next to the three indicates that a high price will be paid for winning. The nine of hearts promises a favorable result. Lower hearts tell us that a contract will be drawn up in a friendly manner and with no disagreement. Lower clubs predict that the client will lead a more active life on account of some document. When such clubs appear, it often signifies that the contract concerns a business alliance which offers your client attractive possibilities.

When low diamonds flank the three of diamonds, the client should take care not to place too much emphasis on meetings about financial matters. As a result of a preoccupation with a lawsuit or conflict about money, a more important opportunity may be lost. In this case, look at the cards in the corners of your spread to see how this conflict can be avoided.

DIAMONDS: possessions,
    financial affairs, the
    spirit of enterprise
FOUR: structure and building
FOUR OF DIAMONDS: financial
    security, concentration
    on certainties

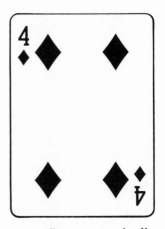

FOUR OF DIAMONDS

Positive: power, rule and order, increasing influence, gradually increasing prosperity, skill in controlling personal use of energy, success, victory

Negative: prejudice, greed, suspiciousness, mundane, regretfulness, restlessness, dissatisfaction

Personal Characteristics

Work is important for all fours, but for the persons signified by the four of diamonds, this is especially true. There is a great need for power, prosperity and security. The four of diamonds is capable of "tunnel vision" when involved in a project that concerns personal success. This concentration needs to be maintained, for if the four loses this focus, poverty or failure may be the result. The possibility of failure does exist for this card, for coupled with the ability to concentrate is the other side of the personality—which includes a need to be free. This innate desire for freedom or liberty can cause a restlessness or dissatisfaction that can interfere with basic career goals.

In addition to the restlessness, the four of diamonds is usually suffering from some problem or other. Most of the problematical trauma can be cured easily, leaving the fours to handle the possibility of being too self-satisfied. This card vascillates between problems and the easy life. The four has a penchant for confusion and incomprehensible developments in regard to relationships for there are many disappointments or miscalculations in both love affairs and business alliances. The four signifies that this individual has the capacity to overcome any unpleasant situations through intelligent insight.

The Card

The four of diamonds indicates concrete, palpable success in the field of finance, business or profession. This is not a card of happiness which suddenly falls out of the sky, coming to the client as a complete surprise. Instead, it indicates progress which comes from personal merit and hard work. Despite the fact that the client tends to underestimate what has been achieved, more satisfaction will be derived by the presence of this card than from more spectacular cards.

Special Significance

A woman having the four of diamonds in a prominent place may either work her way to the top of the professional ladder, or marry a man with plenty of money. She would be motivated by a need for financial security. If she marries for money, she will suffer—the husband will be difficult or she will be bored running a household. She will always pay for unearned financial security by losing personal freedom or happiness.

If the four of diamonds lies in the middle of a spread for a female client, she must beware of relying on feminine charms as the means for getting what she wants. In order to realize her dream, she will have to work hard as she will not get something for nothing. By trusting her own business capabilities, she will not have to compromise her autonomy for financial security.

◆ ◆ ◆

DIAMONDS: possessions, financial affairs, the spirit of enterprise
FIVE: discord, restlessness, change
FIVE OF DIAMONDS: fluctuating financial circumstances

FIVE OF DIAMONDS

Positive: the ability to emerge from life's wretchedness through hard work, building, renovating, common sense and intelligence applied to hard work

Negative: worry, intense strain, inability to act because of a loss of money or a job

Personal Characteristics

The five of diamonds is a card which represent a battle between the idealistic, spiritual desires and a strong interest in personal finances. The five of diamonds may even use idealism as a pretext to avoid a practical point of view. One could interpret this attitude as self-defeating if it were not for the fact that five's innermost ambition is to rise above the mundane to fight for the realization of principles. Until this card has resolved inner conflicts, it is caught in the middle between an opportunistic and an ethical approach to life. Not every five of diamonds suffers from poverty, although most will live on a shoestring budget at some point in life. Financial restrictions may also result from failing health, difficult children, or an environment hostile to the trouble and strain that is borne while this person tries to better personal conditions.

This is an individual who needs to learn to live according to the values which are instinctively recognized as correct. When this is understood, anxiety, cares, and uncertainty can be banished. Although life is not a bed of roses, the five will manage quite well if a purpose or a goal is followed. Since this five is more tolerant and less egotistical than other fives, more responsibility will be shown to family and dependents. The five likes to stay close to the birthplace, and in this case, you may find that our five is unhappily living far from home because of a work situation.

The Card

The five of diamonds signifies a conflict of will between two people. This is not a battle between loved ones or a lasting feud; it is a clash without anger. It may be possible that the problem is not consciously recognized by the people concerned —but the card does symbolize some spiritual conflict between two people who have different moral values and who wish to realize a different future. They may be close and affectionate, but are divided by wishes, dreams or value systems. This could indicate a problem between husband and wife, parent and child, or close friends. Money may play a role here, but it is not the heart of the matter, and should not be allowed to overshadow the real reason causing the strife. The five of diamonds is capable of reaching some kind of agreement, so you can counsel your client that this problem could be worked out in an uncompromising manner. Although the five of diamonds can also indicate new warmth and strength in personal relationships, it also draws attention to the loneliness or separation which may result when the warning contained in the card is disregarded.

Special Significance

If the five of diamonds appears in the middle of a spread, it is an indication that the conflict lies within the client. Several moral viewpoints may be held at the same time, or your client may be torn by indecision with respect to a choice between two differing patterns of life. If this continues, and your client questions successes attained, this inner split may act as a stumbling block to the further realization of personal success or happiness. The client who suspects a hidden struggle which is undermining personal happiness should be advised to clarify motives and desires, putting aside childish grievances while concentrating on more important spiritual values. Once this is comprehended, the values can be made understandable and acceptable to others.

DIAMONDS: possessions, financial affairs, the spirit of enterprise
SIX: meditation, adaptation, understanding of life
SIX OF DIAMONDS: establishing, confronting, the law of cause and effect in practice

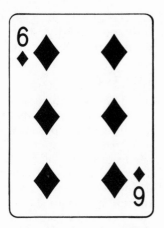

SIX OF DIAMONDS

Positive: success and profit in material affairs, increasing strength, influence, justice, noble-mindedness, philanthropy, dreaminess, vagueness, journeys overland to obtain economic security

Negative: swanky, extravagant, impudent, unwilling, egotistical

Personal Characteristics

Since six is the number associated with a practical attitude toward life, it is obvious that the six of diamonds will represent a person who is levelheaded, and who has a sense of justice. This knowledge is not acquired by birth. In childhood, this person meets intellectual obstacles because the need for money is so primary the six tends to start earning a living before the personal talents have been discovered. The six often starts working even before getting the minimal knowledge so essential for building a successful career.

This is a very strong card. The person described by it learns about justice through experience and self-discipline. The six pays debts on time, honors every obligation or agreement, and is incapable of being insincere. One could say this six is involved with integrity, knowing that values are reflected by position and that we all get what we deserve.

As far as marriage is concerned, the six may have several—or this person may stay married while having several affairs. Love life doesn't always run smoothly because the six will vacillate between being secretive and being open. This person may be moody or seek solace in too much alcohol or drugs. A fulfilling, healthy, and successful life is available as long as values are not sacrificed for possessions.

The Card

The six of diamonds is traditionally seen as a card of health, physical pleasure, and economic security. When it appears in the middle of the spread, it emphasizes the importance of either pleasure or economics. The six can indicate comfortable living conditions, or it can show the client a way to attain this goal. The card suggests that some advantage may be the result of an unforeseen circumstance, or a chance meeting with an old friend. Since a good opportunity may not always be obvious, the client should be warned against hasty decisions, or even against antagonizing some past acquaintance. If the client is presently feeling some aversion to daily employment, a financial opportunity may be missed.

Special Significance

When the six of diamonds lies on a connecting corner or wing of a particular spread, the card often represents a choice between average prosperity (which includes some financial security and peace of mind) and the thrill of an adventurous path that may be strewn with snares or uncertainty. If one of the top corners contains a card that indicates failure, the client should be warned about this. A situation which offers freedom of choice may also put present security at risk. If the six of diamonds is the outside card in a top right corner, it signifies that the goal will be reached if the client stays on the path already chosen. If the six of diamonds is the outside card in the top left corner, it tells us that there will be an opportunity for change which will guarantee the client a safe, protected and comfortable life.

If the six of diamonds is found in a bottom corner, the significance is somewhat altered, for the client needs to become alert in order to make use of a favorable situation. This could be a business transaction which brings a tidy profit, the sale of property, or a period of good fortune during which everything goes well. When a picture card flanks the six of diamonds, this opportunity could be the result of an alliance with someone who exhibits characteristics that relate to the picture card.

A female client with the six of diamonds in the center of a spread should not depend on her charms to grant her success. A male client should avoid spending too much time looking for a rich mate. Someone influenced by this card in a spread is looking for security, but should not sacrifice moral values.

◆ ◆ ◆

DIAMONDS: possessions, financial affairs, the spirit of enterprise
SEVEN: insight, a turning point
SEVEN OF DIAMONDS: disappointment through shortcomings

SEVEN OF DIAMONDS

Positive: gradual development, honorary positions, work undertaken without desire for personal recognition or advancement

Negative: failure, leaving work unfinished, idle speculation, promising enterprises come to nothing, dashed hopes, disappointment, little profit from hard work

Personal Characteristics

The seven of diamonds either represents dissatisfaction, dissappointment, and frustration or the satisfaction and peace of mind that follows the completion of an excellent performance. Anyone ruled by this card will have a personal inner struggle concerning these two extremes. Therefore, this individual may have a one-sided focus on life, or may make life issues into some kind of a compromise between two things—such as prosperity and possessions versus love and relationships, or something of that nature. If emotional and personal ties win out, too little attention may be paid to the material side of life. If all the attention is focussed on attaining prosperity, the personal life may cause problems. And the strain caused by the two factions within the personality may bring periods of total apathy.

This individual needs to have a home, but this may not happen early in life. The domestic atmosphere of childhood may have been subject to many changes, causing the desire for a safe harbor to develop. The seven saves money or makes sacrifices to attain the home, and it should be remembered when reading for a person ruled by this card, that a physical house is an important part of life.

Money is important for the seven of diamonds, but it may also be wasted on trifles. Somehow priorities about spending money may not be really clear. The seven may receive a legacy or marry well to gain financial security, but you may also note that the seven is someone who works hard. Insecurity and a need for financial gain is basically the reason the seven is so industrious. You may even find the seven working in several jobs at the same time.

The person ruled by this card seems to move in cycles of five to seven years. Changes occur in a cyclic rhythm, and the changes are often sudden or violent—not a physical violence—but an upheaval. The changes are received with apprehension, and a good love relationship will alleviate the insecurity felt when the seven moves to unfamiliar ground.

The Card

The seven of diamonds is often a card of sadness and oppression. It represents an unsolved problem about which your client is quite concerned. It usually involves finances, although the problem may also relate to domestic or professional difficulties, with a financial problem somewhere in second place. It may indicate difficulty in regard to making a decision—for the card indicates that circumstances may be obscuring the real issue.

The nature of the problem can be determined from the other cards in the layout. Look for the cards that indicate strength, generosity, moral courage in the face of setbacks, the ability to make friends or receive counsel. The client should be urged to discover how to use these qualities to the best advantage. Strong cards near to the seven of diamonds indicate that the nerve-wracking period will end in achievement. Many times this card signifies that your client cannot listen, for the card indicates a certain tension and desperation. It is important to make your client aware of what talents and traits are available as helpers in the situation.

Special Significance

If the seven of diamonds lies in one of the upper corners of the spread, it means that a trying time lies ahead, but the client can avoid it or keep it under control if the danger is perceived in time. If the seven of diamonds is present in a bottom corner, it is possible that the misfortune could happen to a friend, or circumstances occur that disturb the client's job, commercial occupations, or social endeavors. The seven of diamonds is unique for it indicates not only a problem, but that the client has the wherewithal to find the solution to it.

DIAMONDS: possessions, financial affairs, the spirit of enterprise
EIGHT: power, will, organization
EIGHT OF DIAMONDS: considerable success, management, organization

EIGHT OF DIAMONDS

Positive: moderation and equilibrium, intelligence used for material ends, agriculture, building, career knowledge, craftsmanship, diligence, industry, leadership, respect and prosperity

Negative: calculating, greedy, miserly, pitiless, petty, inability to see the broad perspective, theft, tyranny

Personal Characteristics

All eights possess a capacity for leadership. They all strive for some kind of power, and for the eight of diamonds this power will be taking place in the area of finance. This eight has a greater freedom of choice than eights in other suits. The freedom guaranteed to this eight makes it more independent and sometimes more domineering and demanding than other eights.

The eight of diamonds is very stable. Equilibrium is based on a intuitive sense which allows this individual to know when a good financial prospect is in the offing. Combining intuitive good sense with a strong sense of responsibility, the eight is often found in an executive position. It is easy for this individual to become involved in situations that improve social or financial status, and often committees, meetings with planning boards and directors of organizations include people who are ruled by the eight of diamonds. Because of an inherent stability, the eight of diamonds may be found in trustworthy positions, ranging anywhere from being the guardian of property belonging to others to the lawyer who defends those in need—for a fee of course.

On the other hand, when the eight of diamonds is not functioning from the best of intentions, this individual can be merciless in regard to obtaining financial security. Hunger for power, too much love for money or property, obsessing about the concept of wealth, and even a loss of power can be the result. Should this person be tumbled from a high seat, obligations are forgotten, all sense of responsibility is lost, inheritances entrusted to the eight may be exhausted. Because of the inherent power in the eight, irresponsible behavior will not go unpunished.

The Card

The eight of diamonds is a card if equilibrium and indicates proficiency in financial matters and a healthy perspective in regard to material success. The card represents someone with a practical attitude, for all theories are objectively considered and assimilated. It brings moderation, tolerance, and harmonious power.

Special Significance

When the eight of diamonds appears in a layout dominated by diamonds, the client should be on guard against making purely financial judgments. When the nine or ten of spades follows the eight of diamonds, your client may be seduced into dubious investments by the promise of a quick profit. Advise your client to investigate any financial investments carefully. The presence of clubs in the vicinity of the eight of diamonds will indicate security or a ready income, meaning that your client doesn't have any pressing financial cares. Should the eight of diamonds lie next to a picture card, decisions should not be made by your client without first consulting with an authority in the field under consideration.

If the eight of diamonds lies in the center of the layout, it probably indicates that your client is someone who is capable of looking after business interests without losing either the sense of vision or idealism. This person may be attracted to work involving scientific procedures, or in an important executive position. This person will probably choose a mate who also has an easy but authoritative manner.

If the eight of diamonds appears in the center of a spread done for a female client, she will probably work independently in business. She may marry an employee or a business partner. If she leaves work after marriage, she will usually be the family bookkeeper as well as being a supportive wife and sensible mother.

When the eight of diamonds is in one of the top corners of the layout, a situation will arise that needs careful consideration. Your client should not enter into a decision in haste, for something in the situation needs very close scrutiny.

◆ ◆ ◆

DIAMONDS: possessions, financial affairs, the spirit of enterprise
NINE: desire, the grand passion, philanthropy
NINE OF DIAMONDS: dissatisfaction, intense desires

NINE OF DIAMONDS

Positive: increase, profit, power, liberalism, philanthropy, independence, luck, prosperity

Negative: selfish, covetous, misleading, doubtful, opposing, vague

Personal Characteristics

There seems to be no middle of the road for the person symbolized by this card. The nine is either prosperous, generous and philanthropic; or the nine lives for personal aggrandizement, being incapable of earning the amount of money desired, for this person is often dissatisfied with life. One nine of diamonds type is always fighting to keep head above water, while the more prosperous type battles continually with the dissatisfaction caused by too luxurious a life.

Although the nine has a strong character, there is a tendency for nines to allow themselves to be dominated by others. This happens more often when the nine is very young or very old, or if a strong tie to another person has been developed. Once such alliances are broken, the nine may become a domineering figure in order to regain or maintain a sense of personal freedom. If the nine has been dominated, there is a tendency to avoid marriage. When a relationship eventually does take place, this is the person who can go out for a quart of milk and never return—especially if too much pressure is being directed from the partner.

The nine of diamonds is not generally happy about the idea of marriage, and ventures into marriage or any marriage-type relationship with great care. The nine doesn't really understand that a long term relationship can bring growth with it, for the joy and warmth, the compromise and obligation, even the limitations caused by a relationship can give one a different perspective on life. When the nine falls into an unfulfilling relationship, it may last because it brings a certain form of security with it. This card carries with it a certain kind of rigidity, and although it is considered somewhat independent, it can also be independently aggressive about standing firm in a rut.

The nine of diamonds has sometimes been considered a lucky person whose vague wishes and desires are usually fulfilled. This person may not be aware of the personal motivations that lurk behind behavior patterns. This card is also sometimes indecisive.

The Card

The nine of diamonds is a card with diverse interpretations. Traditionally, it has been called the card of wishes granted, but to the gypsies it symbolizes fraud, treachery, deceit and danger. It has been compared with the pale moonlight which veils reality, for it gives answers which are literally correct, but presents things in a somewhat false light. If the client approaches this card with an open mind, there will be no deception, for the answer always lies in the reading, if the cards are read properly.

Even when your client will not be direct about a particular desire, the cards can be consulted in the hope of finding a solution to some other problem—or the client may merely want to be assured of luck or success in general. The nine of diamonds reflects this unexpressed wish, and predicts that it will be fulfilled to a certain extent. The card indicates that the client may not be expecting what is received, for there is no guarantee that the wish will bring your client either satisfaction or happiness.

Special Significance

The absence of the nine of diamonds doesn't mean that the wish is refused. It simply means that it is not possible to give a conclusive answer in regard to the matter being wished for. If the nine of diamonds is absent, but the nine or ace of spades appear in the spread, it usually indicates an absolute refusal of the wish. If the nine of hearts also plays a part in the reading, the wish remains unfulfilled, but this fact will not cause the client any regret.

If the nine of diamonds and nine of hearts both appear in a layout, luck and good fortune is on its way. The luck will actually surpass the wish, and it will bring your client some new joy in life. Things will be seen in a new light and troubles will disappear like snow in the sun.

If the nine of diamonds occupies an important position in a reading for a female client, it may signify that her husband or lover is addicted to drink or drugs, or that she discovers that her mate is sexually immature, or has unacceptable sexual habits. When the nine of diamonds has an important position when reading for a man, it indicates that relationships will bring him little satisfaction or will cost him too much money or worry. In both cases, the nine of diamonds will be flanked by a picture card, and the surrounding cards will indicate whether the desire for a relationship will be satisfied or not.

If the nine of diamonds lies in the center of the spread, it means that the wish lies very close to the heart, or that some great haste is involved. If the nine is at the top left, the wish may be fulfilled if the client will change something in the present lifestyle. The nine of diamonds in the bottom left corner indicates that the wish is a consequence of other important factors in life, factors over which your client has no control. Should the nine of diamonds be found in one of the outer corners of the spread, it means that the fulfillment of the wish is either impossible or is only going to happen after many delays and setbacks.

◆ ◆ ◆

DIAMONDS: possessions,
    financial affairs, the
    spirit of enterprise
TEN: success, completion
TEN OF DIAMONDS: con-
    sciousness of the value of
    property

TEN OF DIAMONDS

Positive: wealth, luxury, completion on the material plane, steadiness, solidity, maturity, active in business and practical matters

Negative: loss of stimuli in regard to creative goals, loss of vitality, dulling of the mind

Personal Characteristics

The ten of diamonds is considered the most important money card, although this card also indicates a value consciousness. In general, the ten lives according to a normal, conventional, even orthodox pattern. The only ambition may be that of increasing possessions, and this individual runs the risk of being called a moneygrubber.

With respect to financial matters, the ten can do no wrong. Quite apart from the fact that this card appears to have a special sense for making money, legacies may appear from all sides. If the ten should happen to be penniless for a time, or perhaps threatened with the loss of business or property, at the last minute some kind of outside help turns the threatened bankruptcy into an amazing success. The ten prefers to mix with people from "better circles" who enjoy some social status due to prosperity, position in the community, or family origins. The ten is a bit snobbish and wants the world's respect, feeling most comfortable when the environment also radiates prosperity.

In business the ten does well. There is a natural tendency toward business, and large scale projects are never avoided. All business adventures are considered profitable. The individual has a sharp and active intelligence accompanied by a clear view of material values.

Personal life may be affected by moments of doubt. Prosperity can be monotonous and the ten may be overcome by feelings of apathy or boredom. When the lifestyle is questioned in regard to its personal fulfillment, or if personal possessions no longer bring satisfaction, it is time to talk to this person about establishing a new set of values.

The Card

The ten of diamonds indicates either a reduction in personal freedom or some curtailment on the material level. According to gypsy traditions, it is a card that brings luxury but not happiness. The meaning goes even deeper. This card warns against too much emphasis being placed on the pursuit of financial gain, or the possessions that one buys with money. Spiritual needs are neglected. It urges a change in one's spiritual attitude.

When the ten of diamonds appears in a reading, the chances are that your client is already bored, bogged down by routine, or basically indifferent. This person may feel overcome by circumstances and may feel that some dream in regard to spiritual development will never be fulfilled. The card promises that one's future can be changed when the horizons are broadened. Narrow-mindedness is not the order of the day here. Habit, love of ease, fear of change, or apathy will deprive the spirit of its resilience and rob your client of many enjoyable experiences.

Special Significance

The ten of diamonds in the center of a spread is a signal of a diminishing need for self-assertion and an adaptation to a lifestyle that offers material comforts. In other words, deeper fulfillment is missing. A client who has the ten of diamonds in an important position will rise socially due to an alliance with a well-to-do woman. If your client is female, she will either manage a business or own one herself. You could suggest that a richer life lies within reach, but first the client needs to break with the present lifestyle so opportunities offered can be taken. The cards around the ten will tell more about the manner in which the current status can be changed. It should be emphasized that the card indicates that life needs to be seen in a different perspective.

In the bottom corners, the ten of diamonds defines a pleasant interruption of the daily grind. An unexpected gift of money, a journey, or an experience which stimulates some new interest will occur. You should warn your client to take opportunities when they arise or daily routine will take over once again.

◆ ◆ ◆

DIAMONDS: possessions, financial affairs, the spirit of enterprise
JACK: idealism, youth
JACK OF DIAMONDS: a negotiator

JACK OF DIAMONDS

Positive: a young man who devotes energy to practical matters; a competent manager who is inventive but envious of those with more spiritual gifts; someone not quick to anger but when anger is aroused, this person becomes irreconcilable

Negative: extravagant, adulterous, deceitful, boastful, out-of-touch with essential values

Personal Characteristics

The characteristics represented by this card show diversity, unpredictability and ingenuity. The jack of diamonds is unconventional about everything he does. He is very materialistic, but also knows that hard work is necessary to make progress in society, and he is willing to work for what he gets. He needs to be free to move about, and will only work in an atmosphere that includes personal freedom. The jack is original, inventive and hungry for a buck. If he can't find opportunities in his own environment, he will go to another country to make his fortune. Or he might live the life of a vagabond, a lifestyle to which the jack is also suited.

The jack of diamonds likes the water and the sea. Many people with a strong jack of diamonds in a reading will work in relation to the sea in some way. If your client is an ordinary seaman, he may end up as the owner of a shipping line.

The jack of diamonds feels most comfortable in a productive profession because he needs an outlet for creative energy. He can be a good manager, representative, publisher. His need for financial success may block the realization of some natural talents. Once he finds himself, he will play an indispensable part in the structure of his society. This may not happen until later in life, as youth represents a stage of confusion between money and idealism.

The Card

The jack of diamonds represents someone standing at the crossroads of life. When this card appears in the middle of a layout, it can signify either the client or someone who will come to the client for advice or guidance.

The jack of diamonds often refers to a young person, but the card can also reflect maturity rather than just age. It could indicate someone who is torn by inner conflicts for which there are no immediate answers. This person (either male or female) may present a rather reckless impression at first, although in reality the jack seeks a well-balanced and meaningful life. The individual will swing between cynicism and idealism, trying to conceal personal hopes, vision, or even a love of beauty because mockery or condemnation is feared.

The card signifies someone with unmistakable talent who really needs warm friendship and spiritual guidance. The jack may react negatively to any criticism or may be indignant when people don't understand the actions taken. This card may signify one who is thoughtless, irresponsible or even cruel.

The gypsies image of the jack of diamonds is a person hanging between heaven and earth, thereby signifying someone who is upside down, caught between reality and dreams. The jack is strongly introverted and may be incapable of communicating with other people. The jack's position is precarious because the conventional path is avoided like the plague. The card shows someone with a strong tendency to swim against the current and this trait invites resistance or persecution from others, which can eventually break the spirit. If this happens, we are all deprived of the luck that the jack of diamonds can offer. Every attempt to squeeze this card into a conventional mode works the wrong way. It is possible, nonetheless, to direct attention constructively toward a concrete goal, and that can bring balance and success. When the jack senses that ideals are alive in others as well, the sense of isolation is lessened.

Special Significance

If the jack of diamonds is in an outside corner looking outside of the spread, the card indicates someone who will soon disappear from your client's life.

DIAMONDS: possessions, financial affairs, the spirit of enterprise
QUEEN: reacting, judging
QUEEN OF DIAMONDS: business judgment, social involvement

QUEEN OF DIAMONDS

Positive: ambitious, a social climber, energetic, full of will-power, inspiring, friendly, charming, handy, economical

Negative: materialistic, suspicious, critical, nagging, moody, vindictive, proud, foolish, capricious, dissolute, extravagant, unbalanced, malicious

Personal Characteristics

The queen of diamonds is a woman with an intense and passionate temperament. She has plenty of energy and is easily able to assert herself. Her restless spirit is continually filled with plans, schemes, plans for making money, looking for increased respect, or even intervening in someone else's life. She always gets what she wants.

She can be an invaluable friend because she has indomitable courage, and her loyalty remains through thick and thin. She is inspiring to her friends, and sets them to work. Her flair for organization can be used for charitable work, social reform or political interests. She is extremely aggressive and will do anything in her power for those in whom she believes.

At her best, the queen of diamonds is a creative force. Such people bring about progress. When she is included in beneficial projects, her influence can be enormous and her service to mankind of inestimable value. If her interests are developed along constructive lines, and if her friendships are well-made, she will develop more depth and wisdom over the years.

On the other hand, the underdeveloped queen of diamonds can do a great deal of damage if she becomes involved in group work. She is clever and handy, but she may waste her talents. She can become immersed in vulgar quarrels, bitter criticism or just plain gossip. If she becomes involved in misplaced pride, or personal apathy, she runs the risk of not developing the talents that are natural to her. The queen of diamonds needs to learn how to curb her temper in order to stay in control of her passion. She can nurse something into being one day and destroy it with her passion the next, if she doesn't learn how to handle her rage. This is a very powerful woman, and even though she may be underdeveloped when you meet her, she can grow into an incredibly strong force.

The Card

When the queen of diamonds is in the center of a spread, the card describes a female client's personality. It indicates a vital, hard-working and authoritative woman. Although she is prepared to make sacrifices, her sharp tongue may help lose the cause if she is not careful. She may even try to force her will on others just for the excitement of it.

The queen of diamonds holds her destiny in her own hands. She can make her life rich, fruitful, and joyful. She sometimes lacks the patience to develop insight into the motives and feelings of others, and her haste may create enemies.

For the male client, the queen of diamonds indicates a meeting with a woman who has a strong personality. This meeting may have just taken place, or it will happen shortly. Even if this woman is an invaluable ally, she must be handled with kid gloves because she is more sensitive and vulnerable than she seems. If she is offended, she will quickly become an opponent who uses all her knowledge and experience to destroy her enemy. If it is a romantic alliance, she will follow her partner passionately. Tact and friendliness will keep her under control so she can be at her best—challenging and exciting. The man who chooses a queen of diamonds for a wife should not expect a calm and peaceful life. But he will be far from bored!

Special Significance

The queen of diamonds is hostile to the queen of spades. When both appear in the same spread, a clash can be expected. Since the queen of spades is more intuitive and refined, she will probably emerge triumphant. If a skirmish occurs in public, the queen of diamonds is advised to restrain herself and comply if she wishes ot achieve her goal.

There is a certain affinity between the queen of diamonds and the king of clubs. She can bring out the best in him, help him realize his ideals, lend him practical help and assistance, and act as a healthy alternative to his somewhat unbusinesslike attitude. If the layout is dominated by clubs, the queen of diamonds will tend to use her ability well and she can greatly benefit other people.

When diamonds predominate, there is some danger that the queen will be obsessed about money or personal success. A majority of hearts foretells an attitude of benevolence. A predominance of spades generally indicates some heated differences of opinion which can minimize a chance for happiness. If the queen of diamonds appears in any of the corners of a spread and is flanked by a nine or ten of spades, it indicates that the client needs to be warned about falling in love with a woman who may bring sorrow and scandal. If the queen is flanked by the nine of diamonds or the nine of hearts, it indicates that the client may court a woman, or become involved with a woman, who may bring unexpected happiness—but this woman will not be someone who strongly attracts him at the beginning.

DIAMONDS: possessions, financial affairs, the spirit of enterprise
KING: vitality, authority
KING OF DIAMONDS: practical, good business acumen

KING OF DIAMONDS

Positive: intelligent, adept in business matters, great urges to assert himself, generous

Negative: mericiless, excessive, impatient, moody, scheming, jealous, greedy, petty

Personal Characteristics

The king of diamonds symbolizes a man who lives a multifaceted life. He is high-strung, artistic, intelligent, reserved, but hot-tempered—although he can conceal his temper quite well. The king can be sarcastic and this makes him even more enemies. He can be quite creative, and is dominated by a relentless drive, continually throwing himself into new ventures. He has vision and courage, and therefore can do well in business.

He has a mercurial temperament, however. His moods change like the wind, being ecstatic one minute and depressed the next. He can become involved in the art of influence, bribery and intrigue, although he is basically generous and idealistic at the same time. No wonder other people find him confusing!

He can be engagingly friendly, especially to women, as he is usually quite attractive. He can be cold to those who stand in his way, however. He has a strong sense of family unity and cares deeply for children. Although he may look secure to others, he doesn't feel really secure inside, and needs someone who can encourage him, either a confidant or a loyal and understanding partner.

This card symbolizes the born actor—one minute he is inspired, the next morose. When inspired, he forgets family, friends and loved ones. When he is angry he can be merciless. When he is angry, he is very angry, and when his temper cools he is sorry. He usually tries to make up for bad moods by giving grand presents or exaggerated praise. The world is his stage, although he is not drawn to acting. This card could never follow directions!

The Card

When the king of diamonds lies in the center of a spread, the client will exhibit the qualities of the card mentioned above. He will need to learn to channel energy in some constructive direction, avoiding overexcitement and cultivating loyal friendships. This individual needs to avoid excesses.

Warm and intimate relationships are needed by the person symbolized by the king of diamonds, but this is seldom the case in real life. Seldom will this card choose the right mate. A woman who has the characteristics of the queen of spades would be a suitable partner, for her calm intuitive understanding of artistic temperament would be supportive in times of discouragement. However, the king of diamonds is often attracted to the queen of hearts, whose devotion will ultimately bore him, and he cannot rely on the lighthearted queen of clubs.

When the king of diamonds appears in the center for a female client, she will soon be, or may already be, in contact with a gifted and complicated man. Her eyes may also be opened to the ambitions and dreams of a husband, son, admirer or companion. If this is the case, she should try to strengthen her bond with him, for then she will discover that life becomes richer and more meaningful for her.

Special Significance

If the king of diamonds happens to lie on the top left corner in the reading for a female, she will have an opportunity to tie her destiny to the king of diamonds. The opportunity needs to be viewed objectively, for she should consider whether or not her own personality can take second place to that of someone else. She will need to know that her life will become explosive and active. She will have to be steadfast, broadminded and have enough endurance to cópe with the problems that may arise.

She can help such a man reach his peak, but the road will be strewn with disillusionment and heartache. If she should fail, she could cause a lot of pain to both herself and the man she is considering. This is a path to be chosen only by someone who is very strong.

When placed in a top corner for a male client, the king of diamonds indicates a close connection between the client and another man possessing a lively temperament. This could be a friendship, a father-son relationship, or a business partner, although in most cases some intimacy is indicated. The client will play the part of protector or protege to the king of diamonds. This may be a promising and fruitful relationship. Your client should be warned not to fall victim of the other's charisma, for it would not be a good idea to become a puppet in the hands of a stronger personality.

When the king of diamonds lies in a bottom corner, it is a harbinger of either a fine opportunity or a disaster. The cards surrounding the king will determine what the person represented by the king of diamonds has to offer. The client should be careful about acting impulsively in regard to this matter, for it could undermine either family life or social position.

◆ ◆ ◆